A mouthful
of breath mints
and no one to kiss

FIRST THERE WERE CARDS. THEN THERE WERE CARDS AND FLOWERS.

THEN THERE WERE CARDS, FLOWERS AND CANDY. THEN THERE WERE CARDS, FLOWERS, CANDY AND JEWELRY.

NOW THERE ARE CARDS, FLOWERS, CANDY, JEWELRY, TRINKET BOXES, BALLOONS, DESK ACCESSORIES, T-SHIRTS, UNDERWEAR, BOOKS, STICKERS AND SMALL APPLIANCES.

EVERY YEAR THERE ARE MORE THINGS I'M NOT GOING TO GET FOR VALENTINE'S DAY.

IRVING'S DOING IT TO ME, AGAIN, ANDREA. I CAN'T BELIEVE IT!

YAAAA! I'M SO MAD AT YOU, IRVING!

TAKE THAT! AND THAT! AND THAT!!

CATHY, WHY DON'T YOU JUST YELL AT IRVING INSTEAD OF BEATING UP ON YOUR LIVING ROOM?

I DIDN'T HAVE THE ENERGY TO GET INTO A BIG DISCUSSION.

DO YOU THINK I SHOULD SEND DAVID A VALENTINE?

YES, CATHY. DAVID SEEMS LIKE A NICE YOUNG MAN.

WHAT'S THE POINT IN PURSUING A RELATIONSHIP WITH A MAN WHO LIVES HUNDREDS OF MILES AWAY?

THEN, NO. DON'T SEND HIM A VALENTINE.

MOM, HE'S THE MOST UNDERSTANDING MAN I'VE EVER MET!

THEN, YES. BY ALL MEANS, SEND HIM A VALENTINE.

MY MOTHER IS INCAPABLE OF MAKING A DECISION.

PART OF ME DOESN'T EVEN CARE ABOUT VALENTINE'S DAY THIS YEAR... ANOTHER PART OF ME WANTS AN APARTMENT FULL OF CARDS AND FLOWERS...

PART OF ME THINKS VALENTINE'S DAY IS A CHEAP, COMMERCIALIZED EVENT... ANOTHER PART OF ME IS SCREAMING FOR PINK DOILIES AND POETRY...

PART OF ME DOESN'T NEED MY SELF-ESTEEM RAISED BY A VALENTINE... ANOTHER PART OF ME WOULD BEG AND GROVEL FOR ANYTHING WITH A HEART ON IT.

I'LL HAVE THE NACHOS FOR SIX.

QUICK! I ATE THE BOX OF CHOCOLATE MY BOYFRIEND GAVE ME FOR VALENTINE'S DAY AND I HAVE TO REPLACE IT BEFORE HE COMES OVER AND SEES THE EMPTY BOX!

QUICK! I ATE THE BOX OF CHOCOLATE I GOT TO REPLACE THE BOX MY BOYFRIEND GOT ME AND I HAVE TO REPLACE IT AGAIN!

QUICK! I ATE THE BOX OF CHOCOLATE I GOT TO REPLACE THE BOX THAT REPLACED THE BOX MY BOYFRIEND GAVE ME AND I NEED ANOTHER ONE!!

...SORRY I CAN'T MAKE IT OVER, CATHY. I HAVE TO GO OUT OF TOWN FOR A WEEK.

I MIGHT NOT GET A CHANCE TO CALL YOU FROM BOSTON, CATHY, BUT I'LL BE BACK NEXT WEEK. I LOVE YOU.

WHAT?

I'LL BE BACK NEXT WEEK. I LOVE YOU.

YOU WHAT? YOU LOVE ME? IRVING, WHERE ARE YOU?

I'M STANDING IN THE AIRPORT. OOPS. GOTTA GO. BYE.

WHY DON'T YOU EVER SAY YOU LOVE ME WHEN YOU'RE STANDING IN MY LIVING ROOM?!!

WILL THERE BE ANY PROBLEM GETTING REFILLS FOR THIS PHOTO ALBUM?

GOODNESS NO.

THEY'VE BEEN MAKING THESE FOR YEARS.

GREAT. I HATE BUYING SOMETHING AND THEN NOT BEING ABLE TO FIND REFILLS FOR IT.

NO PROBLEM. THAT KIND WILL BE AROUND FOREVER!

THANK YOU VERY MUCH.

YOU CAN STOP PRODUCTION ON THOSE REFILLS NOW.

ATTENTION ALL EMPLOYEES: IN HONOR OF MR. PINKLEY'S BIRTHDAY...

PRODUCT TESTING —INC.—

...THERE USED TO BE A CAKE IN THE COFFEE ROOM.

PRODUCT TESTING —INC.—

I THOUGHT YOU SAID IRVING LOVED THAT DRESS, CATHY.

SOMETIMES PEOPLE SAY THEY LOVE SOMETHING WHEN IT'S HIDEOUS AND THEY DON'T WANT TO HURT YOUR FEELINGS.

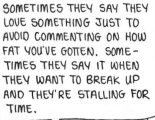
SOMETIMES THEY SAY THEY LOVE SOMETHING JUST TO AVOID COMMENTING ON HOW FAT YOU'VE GOTTEN. SOMETIMES THEY SAY IT WHEN THEY WANT TO BREAK UP AND THEY'RE STALLING FOR TIME.

HOW DOES IRVING FEEL ABOUT THAT DRESS?

HE HATES THIS ONE.

BUT AT LEAST I WON'T HAVE TO WONDER WHAT HE'S THINKING.

IRVING! WELCOME BACK! I MISSED YOU SO MUCH!

CATHY! YOU'RE HERE!

IRVING, PRECIOUS...WOULD YOU MIND DRIVING A TOUCH SLOWER? THE ROADS ARE SO SLIPPERY.

I HAVE IT UNDER CONTROL, HONEY.

IRVING MY DARLING, IF YOU DO NOT SLOW DOWN I AM GOING TO JUMP OUT OF THE CAR AND WALK HOME!!

I AM AN EXCELLENT DRIVER, SWEETHEART!!

JUST ONCE I WISH A RELATIONSHIP WOULD LAST ALL THE WAY HOME FROM THE AIRPORT.

YOU KNOW WHAT'S WRONG WITH RELATIONSHIPS, ANDREA?...KITCHENS!

WHO COOKS...WHO CLEANS UP...THESE MEANINGLESS QUESTIONS UNDERMINE THE BEST OF ROMANCES.

IT'S A **RELIEF** TO GO TO THE OFFICE WHERE **NO ONE CARES** ABOUT WHAT HAPPENS IN THE STUPID KITCHEN!!!

ON THE TOP OF OUR AGENDA TODAY IS "KITCHEN DUTY."

YAAAK! JUST A SECOND! OKAY! WAIT! YAAACK! OKAY, OKAY, JUST A SECOND! WAIT!!

COME ON, CATHY. IT'S AFTER 6:30.

IT LOOKS LIKE A LITTLE ANGEL WHEN IT'S SLEEPING.

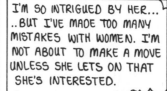

HI. I'M DANIEL. HOW DO YOU FEEL ABOUT THE WHOLE MEN/WOMEN THING?

ARE YOUR BELIEFS STRONGER THAN YOUR ACTIONS OR VICE VERSA? IF YOU HAD A DAUGHTER RIGHT NOW, WOULD YOU CONSIDER YOURSELF A GOOD ROLE MODEL?

WHICH AUTHORS HAVE BEST CAPTURED HOW YOU FEEL? ARE YOUR RELATIONSHIPS MORE COMPLICATED NOW AND IF SO, IS IT PARTLY BECAUSE IT'S HARDER TO SAY YOU NEED SOMEONE WITHOUT APPEARING TO BE A HYPOCRITE?

WHATEVER HAPPENED TO "HELLO, BEAUTIFUL. WHAT'S YOUR SIGN?"

YES, OF COURSE, MR. PINKLEY.

NO PROBLEM. I'M SURE THE TIME YOU SPEND WILL ULTIMATELY BE A BENEFIT TO THE CORPORATE IMAGE.

CERTAINLY... AS THE HEAD OF THIS DIVISION, IT'S CRUCIAL FOR YOU TO STAY ON TOP OF NEW DEVELOPMENTS SUCH AS THIS. I UNDERSTAND.

MR. PINKLEY WILL BE A LITTLE LATE TODAY. HE'S HAVING HIS COLORS DONE.

WHAT DOES "CRAB BORDELAISE" MEAN?

IT'S FRENCH FOR CELLULITE.

MOM, IF YOU'RE UPSET ABOUT SOMETHING, WOULD YOU JUST SAY WHAT IT IS?!

WELL. AREN'T WE GROUCHY TODAY?

I'M NOT GROUCHY. I JUST WISH YOU'D OPEN UP AND SAY WHAT'S ON YOUR MIND FOR ONCE!!

WHAT'LL IT BE, LADIES?

THE CRAB AND THE CLAM.

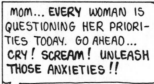

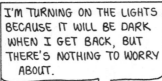

MY FRIEND OLLIE WROTE TO THE GOVERNMENT FOR INFORMATION ON SMALL BUSINESS SUBSIDIES.

FLO ORDERED BROCHURES ON SETTING UP SMALL BUSINESSES AND FINANCING BUSINESSES. HELEN SENT IN FOR "SMALL BUSINESS STRATEGIES," "BUSINESS STATISTICS" AND "YOUR BUSINESS AND YOU".

TOMORROW WE'RE GOING TO SIT DOWN AND START TURNING OUR DREAMS INTO REALITY!

GOOD FOR YOU, MOM!

WE HAVE TO. WE RAN OUT OF THINGS TO SEND AWAY FOR.

FLO, WE HAVE GATHERED HERE TO DISCUSS NEW BUSINESS OPPORTUNITIES... NOT TO LISTEN TO YOU GLOAT ABOUT YOUR GRANDDAUGHTER.

IF YOU WHIP OUT THAT PHOTO ALBUM ONE MORE TIME, I WILL HAVE NO CHOICE BUT TO DISMISS YOU FROM THIS AND ALL FURTHER SESSIONS... ALL IN FAVOR, SAY "AYE!"

OH, SHE'S ADORABLE ...OOH, LOOK AT THIS ONE

OOH... ISN'T THAT SWEET... AW...

MOVE OVER, OLLIE.

IF YOUR CATHY WERE MARRIED LIKE MY DAUGHTERS...

FLO, I HAPPEN TO BE VERY PROUD OF CATHY'S INDEPENDENCE.

WHEN AND IF SHE DECIDES TO MARRY AND HAVE A FAMILY, SHE WILL BE DOING SO ON A SOLID FOUNDATION OF CONFIDENCE AND SELF-RESPECT!

MOM, I COULDN'T HELP OVERHEARING WHAT YOU SAID. THAT WAS BEAUTIFUL!

WHERE ARE MY GRANDCHILDREN??

FLO, WAIT! COME BACK!

Panel 1: I'M HERE! I FLOODED THE LAUNDRY ROOM...I SHORTED-OUT MY HAIRDRYER...I DUMPED THE COFFEE POT IN MY BRIEFCASE...I RIPPED MY HEM...

GATE 72 GATE

Panel 2: ...AND I HAD TO LEAVE MY CAR STRANDED ON THE FREEWAY, BUT I'M HERE! I OVERCAME EVERY CRISIS AND GOT HERE ON TIME!!

Panel 3: THERE ARE 38 PLANES AHEAD OF US ON THE RUNWAY. WE SHOULD BE TAKING OFF IN ABOUT 2½ HOURS.

2½ HOURS?? I CAN'T BELIEVE IT!

Panel 4: I HAD TIME TO BREAK FIFTEEN MORE THINGS.

Panel 5: I'M GOING TO TRANSFER MY SAVINGS TO A LONG-TERM, HIGH-INTEREST ACCOUNT AND THAT'S THAT!

Panel 6: ...BUT WHAT IF I DECIDE TO BUY A HOUSE THIS YEAR? WHAT IF I HAVE TO ACT FAST ON A HOT STOCK TIP? WHAT IF I WANT TO TAKE A WORLD CRUISE??

Panel 7: YES! I MIGHT TAKE A WORLD CRUISE...GO INTO LAND DEVELOPMENT WITH ONE OF THE PASSENGERS... ..SHE'LL INTRODUCE ME TO..YAAA! I CAN'T HAVE MY MONEY LOCKED UP!!

Panel 8: WHAT DID YOU DO WITH YOUR $500, CATHY?

NOTHING. BY THE TIME IT WAS MY TURN, I NEEDED IT TO REDECORATE THE BABY'S ROOM.

SAVINGS & LOAN

Panel 9: I'D BETTER GO. THIS CALL IS COSTING YOU A FORTUNE, CATHY.

OH, DON'T WORRY ABOUT IT, MARY...

Panel 10: ...I'VE OWED YOU A LETTER FOR SIX MONTHS!

YOU STILL OWE ME A LETTER.

Panel 11: WHAT DO YOU MEAN, I STILL OWE YOU A LETTER?? I JUST TALKED TO YOU LONG DISTANCE FOR TWO HOURS!!

PHONE CALLS DON'T CANCEL OUT LETTER DEBTS. ONLY LETTERS CANCEL LETTER DEBTS.

Panel 12: AFTER SIX MONTHS, PEOPLE START TO TURN ON YOU.

SOMETIMES I GET THE FEELING THAT I'M JUST WANDERING AROUND BETWEEN LADIES' ROOMS, ANDREA.

I GO TO WORK...I GO CHECK MY OUTFIT IN THE LADIES' ROOM..I GO TO A MEETING.. ..I GO CHECK MY HAIR IN THE LADIES' ROOM...

BEFORE, DURING AND AFTER EVERY EVENT OF MY LIFE, I MAKE THIS RITUALISTIC STOP IN THE LADIES' ROOM!

WELL, WHAT ARE YOU GOING TO DO TO CHANGE IT, CATHY?

I THINK MAYBE I'LL JUST STAY IN HERE.

I'M SORRY I MISSED THE PARTY LAST NIGHT, IRVING.

I KNOW IT WAS IMPORTANT TO YOU, BUT I PROMISED MR. PINKLEY I'D WORK LATE.

CATHY, THOSE PEOPLE ARE ABUSING YOU.

MR. PINKLEY CONTROLS YOUR WHOLE LIFE! AND YOU KNOW WHAT? HE'S GOING TO KEEP ON DOING IT IF YOU DON'T DEMAND A LIFE OF YOUR OWN.

I KNOW, HONEY...LOOK, I'LL MAKE IT UP TO YOU TONIGHT.

I CAN'T. I HAVE TO WORK LATE.

"NOTICE TO ALL CUSTOMERS: ALL DRESSING ROOMS IN THIS STORE MAY BE MONITORED FOR SECURITY REASONS."

WHAT IS THE MEANING OF THIS SIGN??

OH, DON'T WORRY ABOUT IT.

THAT'S JUST UP THERE TO SCARE OFF SHOPLIFTERS.

THAT'S A RELIEF.

HERE...THIS WASN'T QUITE WHAT I WAS LOOKING FOR.

GOOD DECISION. I THOUGHT IT LOOKED RIDICULOUS ON YOU.

I TOLD JOAN HER BOY-FRIEND WAS TAKING ADVANTAGE OF HER AND THAT SHE SHOULD DUMP HIM.

THEN JOAN TOLD ME MY BOYFRIEND WAS TAKING ADVANTAGE OF ME AND THAT I SHOULD DUMP HIM.

THEN WE SCREAMED AT EACH OTHER FOR NOT UNDERSTANDING AND WENT HOME TO OUR BOYFRIENDS.

WE'RE GETTING BETTER AT CONFRONTING EACH OTHER'S PROBLEMS.

IT'S MY PRIVILEGE TO PRESENT YOU WITH A RAISE TODAY, CATHY.

YOU'RE DEVOTED, ENTHUSIASTIC, RESPONSIBLE, PRODUCTIVE AND INNOVATIVE.

WE ALL KNOW YOU DESERVE A RAISE... YET, I THINK YOU'LL FIND THIS SUM BEYOND YOUR WILDEST EXPECTATIONS...

2 MILLION DOLLARS !!

I FORGOT WHO I WAS DEALING WITH.

I GOT A RAISE, IRVING! I GOT A RAISE AND I DIDN'T EVEN HAVE TO BEG FOR IT !!

I AM FINALLY NEEDED, APPRECIATED, **AND** REWARDED! OH, IRVING, I WANT TO SAVOR THIS MOMENT **FOREVER** !!

I'M THRILLED FOR YOU, CATHY. I GOT LAID OFF TODAY.

I WAS HOPING FOREVER WOULD LAST LONGER THAN THAT.

I'M HAPPY TO FORMALLY ANNOUNCE CATHY'S PROMOTION TO THE LOWER RUNG OF MANAGEMENT AT PRODUCT TESTING, INC.

OH, NO. NOT TODAY. NO..NO!

CATHY'S UNWAVERING COMMITMENT TO WHAT SHE BELIEVES IN MAKES HER A LEADER WE CAN ALL TURN TO FOR FOCUS AND STRENGTH... ..CATHY, HOW ABOUT A FEW WORDS?

THE SALES CLERK MADE ME BUY IT.

IRVING GOT LAID OFF AND I GOT A PROMOTION. WHAT DO I SAY TO REASSURE HIM??

WHY DON'T YOU SEND HIM A NICE BALLOON-O-GRAM?

MY GENERATION HAPPENS TO BELIEVE IN TALKING, MOM. WE CONFRONT OUR FEELINGS.

DING DONG!

WHY COULDN'T YOU HAVE GOTTEN LAID OFF LAST MONTH, WHEN I HAD TIME TO COPE WITH IT??

WE CONFRONT OUR FEELINGS. THEN WE SEND A BALLOON-O-GRAM.

THEY'VE ALL SEEN MY PICTURE BY NOW, AND THEY'VE ALL READ ABOUT MY BIG PROMOTION.

THEY'RE PROBABLY ALL LOOKING AT ME... MAYBE THEY'RE EVEN A LITTLE INTIMIDATED.

OH, BUT THAT'S SO SILLY... I'M THE SAME PERSON I ALWAYS WAS. HA, HA! I'M APPROACHABLE... I'M GRACIOUS ...MY AUTOGRAPH? OH..WELL, OF COURSE I'LL TAKE THE TIME...

IT'S HARD TO BE HUMBLE WHEN NOBODY READS THE COMPANY NEWSLETTER.

UP
down

MOM, WHAT ARE YOU GOING TO DO WITH 900 COPIES OF THE COMPANY NEWSLETTER THAT HAS MY PICTURE IN IT?

I'M GOING TO TAKE THEM DOWN TO THE SHOPPING MALL, SET UP A LITTLE BOOTH OUTSIDE THE HOT PRETZEL STAND AND FORCE PERFECT STRANGERS TO READ ABOUT YOU!

OH... I'M SORRY, MOM. I DIDN'T MEAN TO INSULT YOU. YOU CAN HAVE AS MANY COPIES AS YOU WANT.

WHAT DID SHE THINK I WAS GOING TO DO WITH THEM?

"Read about my daughter"

WHAT'S ON TV TONIGHT, CATHY?

LET'S SEE... THERE'S A 92-YEAR-OLD MAN WHO TRAINED HIS COCKROACHES TO PLAY MOZART CONCERTOS...

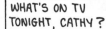

...A WOMAN WHO CLAIMS SHE CAN EAT A 7-PIECE PATIO SET IN 45 MINUTES... A 3-YEAR OLD WHO BUILT A MICROWAVE OVEN OUT OF PLAYPEN PARTS...

...A COW IN MILWAUKEE THAT SAVED A FAMILY OF 12...AND A GRANDMOTHER WHO DOES A TRAMPOLINE ACT OVER A PIT OF WILD BOARS.

EH... SAME OLD STUFF.

HI! MAY I HELP YOU FIND SOMETHING FOR YOUR STUNNINGLY PETITE FIGURE?

I'M JUST LOOKING, THANKS.

FINE. IF YOU NEED HELP, JUST ASK ME. I'M MARGARET. YOUR HAIR IS JUST LOVELY. WANT ME TO PUT THAT IN A DRESSING ROOM FOR YOU?

NO. I WAS JUST LOOKING AT IT.

TAKE YOUR TIME. JUST REMEMBER ME. MARGARET. THAT COLOR WOULD BE BEAUTIFUL AGAINST YOUR FLAWLESS COMPLEXION.

MARGARET, I SWEAR I WON'T LET ANYONE ELSE WAIT ON ME!!

WHERE'S MARGARET?

SHE WENT OUT TO LUNCH.

DRESSING ROOMS

NO ONE ADMITTED WITHOUT A SALESPERSON.

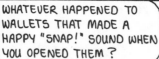

WHATEVER HAPPENED TO WALLETS THAT MADE A HAPPY "SNAP!" SOUND WHEN YOU OPENED THEM?

PASSE. WE'RE INTO VELCRO NOW. IT RIPS OPEN.

WALLETS RIP!

SEE? -RIP!- THE VELCRO "RIIIP!" IS THE LOOK AND THE SOUND OF THE 80'S SHOPPER.

IT SOUNDS LIKE THE WALLET IS SCREAMING EVERY TIME YOU OPEN IT.

RIIP!

PRECISELY. AND IT CAN BE YOURS FOR JUST $21.95.

YAAAA!

RIP!

I SEE YOUR POINT.

HO, HUM. I THINK YOU'D BETTER TAKE ME HOME, EDWARD.

OKAY, CATHY.

YOU'RE KIDDING. YOU'RE NOT GOING TO HASSLE ME ABOUT STAYING? NO BEGGING? NO SNEAK ATTACKS? NO "HOW ABOUT A QUICK BACK MASSAGE, HONEY?"?

DON'T BE SILLY. LET'S GO.

OH, EDWARD, I LOVE YOU FOR THIS!!!

KISS
KISS
KISS

HEH, HEH, HEH...

TAKE ME HOME, EDWARD.

HI, CATHY. ARE YOU IN THE MIDDLE OF ANYTHING?

IT'S APRIL 10, ANDREA. OF COURSE I'M IN THE MIDDLE OF SOMETHING.

WILL YOU BE BUSY ALL EVENING?

IT'S APRIL 10. OF COURSE I'LL BE BUSY ALL EVENING.

WHAT ARE YOU DOING?

ANDREA, IT'S APRIL 10. WHAT DO YOU THINK I'M DOING??!

Dear Aunt Dorothy, Thank you for the lovely scarf you sent for Christmas...

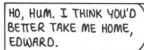

YOU'RE WORKING TOO HARD, CATHY. WHY DON'T YOU GO FRESHEN UP?

A LITTLE SPLASH OF WATER CAN BE AS REFRESHING AS A SHORT NAP.

ONCE AN OVER-ACHIEVER, ALWAYS AN OVER-ACHIEVER.

TOWE

I'VE BEEN SO BUSY...THANKS FOR HELPING WITH MY TAX RETURNS, IRVING.

NO PROBLEM. FOR EVERY NIGHT YOU'VE WORKED LATE, I SIMPLY ADDED $300 TO YOUR "AMOUNT DUE".

FORMS

I ADDED $450 FOR REFUSING TO DO MY LAUNDRY, AND $475 FOR REFUSING TO COOK MY DINNER.

I ADDED $1200 FOR THAT WEEKEND YOU SPENT IN ST. LOUIS WITH THAT TWERP ...AND 75¢ FOR EACH TIME IN 1981 THAT YOU SAID "I HATE FOOTBALL."

SO FAR, YOU OWE THE GOVERNMENT $26,000.00.

SINGLE PEOPLE ARE ALWAYS THE HARDEST HIT AT TAX TIME.

THANKS FOR COMING, CATHY. LIKE OUR AD SAYS, WE ARE THE COMPLETE TAX PREPARATION CENTER.

THE COMPLETE TAX PREP CENTER

WE EXAMINE YOUR TAX HISTORY... WE DIG FOR EVERY DEDUCTION... WE SCRUTINIZE EVERY CLAUSE...WE SEARCH OUT EACH AND EVERY LOOPHOLE!

SHOULDN'T THAT HAVE TAKEN MORE THAN THREE MINUTES?

I PAID MY INCOME TAXES.

IF I SELL ALL MY POSSESSIONS, QUIT USING ELECTRICITY AND GAS, CHOP MY FURNITURE UP FOR FIREWOOD...

...AND START SEWING MY OWN CLOTHES OUT OF OLD BEDSPREAD MATERIAL, I HAVE A CHANCE OF BREAKING EVEN THIS YEAR.

I'M STARTING TO SEE WHY THE "PRAIRIE LOOK" IS IN.

DID YOU SEE THIS, ANDREA? ...IF I LEAVE MY PANS AND COOKING UTENSILS LYING AROUND ON THE COUNTER, I LOOK LIKE A SLOB.

HOWEVER, IF I HANG THESE SAME PANS AND SPATULAS FROM THE CEILING AND WALLS, I INSTANTLY CREATE THE LOOK OF A GOURMET COOK!

PANS ON THE COUNTER: SLOB. PANS HANGING FROM THE CEILING: SOPHISTICATE. HA, HA! IT'S SO EASY!!

YOU'RE SUPPOSED TO WASH THEM FIRST, CATHY.

THERE'S ALWAYS A CATCH...

YOU ALWAYS SAID IT WOULDN'T MATTER WHICH ONE OF US WAS MAKING MORE MONEY, REMEMBER?

SO WHAT IF I GOT A PROMOTION? SO WHAT THAT YOU'RE LAID OFF?

IRVING, WE'RE TWO PEOPLE WHO LOVE EACH OTHER! WHAT DIFFERENCE DOES MONEY MAKE??!

THE LADY'S BUYING.

THAT'LL BE $78.00.

WAIT A MINUTE...

HI. I'M CALLING ABOUT THE TOP LEVEL MANAGEMENT POSITION YOU HAVE OPEN.

SORRY. THAT POSITION HAS BEEN FILLED BY A DONKEY-KONG GAME.

WITH JUST A FEW VIDEO GAMES, WE FIGURE WE CAN BRING IN THE KIND OF BIG BUCKS THAT A WHOLE OFFICE FULL OF TOP MANAGEMENT COULDN'T PRODUCE.

IS THAT SO ?! WELL, I'D LIKE TO HEAR THAT FROM THE PRESIDENT !!

SORRY. HE'S UNDERGOING REPAIRS RIGHT NOW.

WHAT DO YOU MEAN, THE JOB IS FILLED ? THE NEWSPAPER JUST CAME OUT FOURTEEN SECONDS AGO !

DO YOU HAVE ANY IDEA HOW MANY CALLS I'VE MADE ? DO YOU HAVE ANY IDEA HOW MUCH I HATE BEGGING SOME TWERP TO GLANCE AT MY RESUME ??

YOU WANT TO KNOW WHY I DON'T HAVE A JOB ?? BECAUSE THE WORLD IS FULL OF YO-YO'S LIKE YOU !

LOOK ON THE BRIGHT SIDE, IRVING.

AT LEAST YOU DON'T WORK IN THE PERSONNEL DEPARTMENT.

I WAS REJECTED BY 47 MORE COMPANIES TODAY, CATHY. WANT TO HAVE DINNER?

UM...THAT ALL DEPENDS, IRVING.

WILL YOU ALWAYS LOVE ME FOR STANDING BY YOU IN YOUR TIME OF NEED.... OR WILL YOU RESENT ME FOR BEING THE ONE PERSON WHO SAW YOU DURING THIS MISERABLE PERIOD OF YOUR LIFE ?

...I SEE. OH, IRVING, ISN'T THAT SWEET ?

HE WANTS IT TO BE A SURPRISE.

♪ HI, IRVING! LOOK AT THIS GREAT JOB-HUNTING GUIDE I FOUND FOR YOU!! ♪ ♪

CATHY, DO YOU HAVE ANY IDEA HOW ANNOYING IT IS FOR A MAN TO HAVE HIS GIRLFRIEND CHEERFULLY LEAPING AROUND WHILE HE'S ON THE BRINK OF DISASTER?

MOTHERS CHEERFULLY LEAP AROUND. GIRLFRIENDS DO NOT CHEERFULLY LEAP AROUND.

WHAT DID I DO NOW?

I'M SO BUSY, I DON'T HAVE TIME TO EAT.

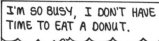

I'M SO BUSY, I DON'T HAVE TIME TO EAT A DONUT.

I'M SO BUSY, I DON'T HAVE TIME TO EAT A DONUT COVERED WITH GOOEY CHOCOLATE FROSTING.

I'M TOO BUSY TO BE ON A DIET.

IF I WEAR THE OUTFIT I LOOK BEST IN ON MY FIRST DATE WITH THIS MAN, I WON'T HAVE ANYTHING TO WEAR IF I EVER GO OUT WITH HIM AGAIN.

THEN AGAIN, IF I DON'T WEAR WHAT I LOOK BEST IN, I'LL BE UNCOMFORTABLE ALL NIGHT, I'LL ACT WEIRD, AND THERE WON'T BE A SECOND DATE.

THEN AGAIN, IF I WEAR THE GREAT OUTFIT AND WE HAVE A WONDERFUL TIME, I'LL HAVE TO BUY A WHOLE NEW WARDROBE TO LIVE UP TO THE FIRST IMPRESSION I MADE.

I DECIDED TO STAY HOME AND WATCH TV.

Panel 1: HI, IRVING. WOULD YOU MIND PICKING UP MY DRY CLEANING TODAY?

Panel 2: CATHY, JUST BECAUSE I'M NOT GOING INTO A REGULAR OFFICE DOESN'T MEAN I HAVE NOTHING TO DO.

Panel 3: I HAVE INTERVIEWS TO SET UP... CALLS TO MAKE... RESUMES TO PREPARE... I DO NOT HAVE TIME TO RUN AROUND DOING YOUR ERRANDS!

Panel 4: PEOPLE WHO WORK AT HOME GET NO RESPECT.

QUACK!

Panel 5: I'D LIKE A BREATH MINT, BUT I DON'T WANT TO BE SO OBVIOUS ABOUT PREPARING FOR A BIG KISS AT THE DOOR.

Panel 6: I COULD OFFER HIM A BREATH MINT, BUT THEN I'D BE REALLY OBVIOUS... I COULD TRY TO SECRETLY EAT A BREATH MINT, BUT THAT WOULD BE REALLY, REALLY OBVIOUS... I..

BYE, CATHY. SEE YOU SOON.

Panel 7:

Panel 8: THE STORY OF MY LIFE. A MOUTHFUL OF BREATH MINTS, AND NO ONE TO KISS.

Panel 9: EVERYWHERE YOU GO, THERE'S TOO MUCH STUFF TO BUY. I WENT TO THE DRUGSTORE FOR A TUBE OF TOOTHPASTE, I CAME OUT WITH A DINETTE SET.

Panel 10: I WENT TO THE GAS STATION FOR GAS, I CAME HOME WITH A 5-PIECE LUGGAGE ENSEMBLE.

Panel 11: I WENT TO THE CARD SHOP FOR A CARD, I CAME AWAY WITH AN ESPRESSO MACHINE. YOUR FATHER IS JUST GOING TO KILL ME.

WHERE **IS** DAD?

Panel 12: HE RAN OUT FOR A NEWSPAPER.

OOH, IRVING, LET'S GO HEAR JAMES LEE STANLEY PLAY.

FORGET IT, CATHY. I KNOW HOW WOMEN ARE.

THE GUY SINGS A FEW SONGS... YOU GAZE AT HIS FACE... YOU GET CAUGHT UP IN HIS LYRICS... AND BY THE END OF ONE SET, YOU'RE LOOKING AT ME LIKE I HAVE CROSSED EYES.

I AM SICK OF PAYING TEN BUCKS SO MY DATE CAN FALL IN LOVE WITH SOME MUSICIAN!!

FINE. WHAT DO YOU WANT TO DO TONIGHT?

LET'S SEE IF OLIVIA NEWTON-JOHN IS IN TOWN.

WHERE HAVE YOU BEEN ALL EVENING, CATHY??

I WENT TO HEAR JAMES LEE STANLEY. YOU DIDN'T WANT TO GO IRVING, REMEMBER?

IT WAS GREAT, IRVING. MY SEAT WAS PERFECT... THE SONGS WERE WONDERFUL... THE MUSIC WAS TREMENDOUS...

THE AUDIENCE WAS SCREAMING FOR ENCORES... IT WAS ONE OF THE FINEST EVENINGS OF MY LIFE!!

DID YOU MISS ME, HONEY?

THE HOT NEW LOOK FOR SPRING IS THE LONG, FLOWERY, RUFFLED PRAIRIE LOOK.

THE HOT NEW LOOK IS ALSO FLASHY STRIPES WITH FAT PUNK BELTS... AND THE HOT NEW LOOK IS PASTEL MILITARY MINI-SKIRTS. THEY ARE ALL THE HOT NEW LOOK.

THESE ARE TOTALLY DIFFERENT THINGS. THEY CAN'T ALL BE THE HOT NEW LOOK.

THEY ARE ALL EQUALLY THE HOT NEW LOOK!

IT LOOKS LIKE ANOTHER GOOD YEAR TO BUY SHOES.

WAIT UP.

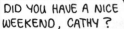

Panel 1:
DID YOU HAVE A NICE WEEKEND, CATHY?

YES, MR. PINKLEY. I WENT TO THE SYMPHONY WITH A MAN I JUST MET.

Panel 2:
HE OPENED MY EYES TO A WHOLE NEW WORLD AND MADE ME REALIZE HOW TRIVIAL AND MEANINGLESS MY BUSINESS PROBLEMS ARE.

Panel 3:
THIS IS STUPID, BORING, DISGUSTING WORK, MR. PINKLEY. MY JOB MAKES ME SICK!!

Panel 4:
...NEVER REPORT ON YOUR WEEKEND BEFORE YOU'VE HAD YOUR COFFEE.

Panel 5:
I CANNOT BELIEVE YOU SPENT MORE MONEY ON CLOTHES, CATHY.

ACCESSORIES, IRVING.

Panel 6:
ACCESSORIES ARE THE KEY FOR THE SMART 80's SHOPPER.

WHAT DID YOU GET TALKED INTO NOW?

Panel 7:
...WITH JUST ONE VERSATILE SCARF, I CAN SOLVE ALL MY WARDROBE PROBLEMS!!

HAH!

Panel 8:
HM! IT WORKS BETTER THAN I THOUGHT.

Panel 9:
I AM TOTALLY ATTRACTED TO THIS MAN, AND I WANT HIM TO KNOW IT.

Panel 10:
IT'S TIME WOMEN LEARNED TO TAKE THE INITIATIVE AND TAKE A CHANCE!

Panel 11:
THERE! I'VE DONE IT! MY FEELINGS ARE KNOWN AND IT'S UP TO HIM TO REACT!!

Panel 12:
WHAT DID YOU SAY TO LET THIS MAN KNOW YOU WERE SO INTERESTED, CATHY?

MY ELBOW TOUCHED HIS ARM.

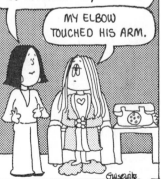

MY BLUE SKIRT AND MY TAN JACKET ARE GETTING DRY CLEANED.

MY GREEN DRESS IS HAVING A NEW ZIPPER PUT IN. MY LAVENDER BLOUSE IS WAITING FOR BUTTONS.

MY WHITE SLACKS AND ALL MY UNDERWEAR ARE IN THE WASHING MACHINE.

I WON'T BE IN TODAY, MR. PINKLEY. MY CLOTHES ARE ALL BUSY.

I KNOW UNEMPLOYMENT IS HARD ON YOU, IRVING, BUT I DON'T WANT IT TO DRIVE US APART.

YOUR TRIUMPHS ARE **OUR** TRIUMPHS... YOUR DISASTERS ARE **OUR** DISASTERS...

IRVING, IF WE CAN JUST LEARN TO SHARE, NOTHING WILL EVER COME BETWEEN US!!

RING RING

...IT'S OUR OTHER GIRLFRIEND.

14 RINGS...15 RINGS... COME ON, IRVING, ANSWER YOUR PHONE.

RING! RING!

19...20...21...I KNOW YOU'RE THERE, IRVING, AND I'M GOING TO LET IT RING UNTIL I TALK TO YOU!

RING! RING!

CATHY, EXACTLY HOW GOOD OF A CONVERSATION DO YOU EXPECT TO HAVE WITH A MAN WHO'S LET HIS PHONE RING 26 TIMES BEFORE ANSWERING IT ??

RING RING RING

....HELLO?

GLFKT.

YOU MADE ME NERVOUS.

NO, I WILL NOT STAY LATE AGAIN, MR. PINKLEY. MY PERSONAL RELATIONSHIPS ARE UNDER A BIG ENOUGH STRAIN WITHOUT ADDING ANOTHER MIDNIGHT AT THE OFFICE.

IF YOU CONTINUE TO MAKE THESE OUTRAGEOUS DEMANDS, YOU'RE GOING TO HAVE TO JUST FIND YOURSELF ANOTHER SLAVE!

IT'S HARD TO BELIEVE I PUT MY CAREER ON THE LINE FOR A "THREE'S COMPANY" RERUN.

WELL, UM, MAYBE WE CAN GET TOGETHER SOMETIME, CATHY... MAYBE I'LL GIVE YOU A CALL NEXT WEEK... MAYBE WE'LL GET SOME DINNER... WELL, MAYBE. WE'LL SEE...

MEN ARE LUNATICS, ANDREA.

YOU JUST EXPECT TOO MUCH, CATHY.

WHEN ARE YOU GOING TO REALIZE THERE'S NO SUCH THING AS "MR. RIGHT"?

ANDREA, I KNOW THERE'S NO SUCH THING AS MR. RIGHT.

...THEY'RE ALL MR. MAYBE'S.

I'M WEARING "THE PROVOCATIVE NEW COLOGNE FOR WOMEN." HE'S WEARING "THE DARING NEW MEN'S COLOGNE."

THE ROOM IS CHARGED WITH ELECTRICITY.

I THINK OUR COLOGNES ARE HAVING A PARTY IN MID-AIR.

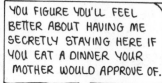

YOU HEARD ME, IRVING. I WANT LIVER FOR DINNER.

EVERY TIME YOU FEEL GUILTY ABOUT SOMETHING, YOU START WORRYING ABOUT YOUR NUTRITION.

YOU FIGURE YOU'LL FEEL BETTER ABOUT HAVING ME SECRETLY STAYING HERE IF YOU EAT A DINNER YOUR MOTHER WOULD APPROVE OF.

YOU'RE NUTS, CATHY! NOBODY IN THE WORLD IS AS NUTS AS YOU ARE!!

AT LEAST I KNOW SHE'S EATING RIGHT.

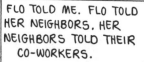

HOW DID YOU FIND OUT THAT IRVING IS STAYING AT MY APARTMENT, MOM?

FLO TOLD ME.

FLO TOLD ME. FLO TOLD HER NEIGHBORS. HER NEIGHBORS TOLD THEIR CO-WORKERS.

THEIR CO-WORKERS ALERTED ALL THEIR RELATIVES, WHO SET UP A COAST-TO-COAST HOTLINE... AND FOR THOSE WHO MISSED OUT, STAY TUNED FOR THE 6:00 NEWS!

... THAT'S THE LAST TIME I ASK FLO TO SNEAK OVER TO YOUR PLACE AND FIND OUT WHAT'S GOING ON.

IRVING, YOUR DIRTY DISHES ARE IN MY SINK!

SO WHAT, CATHY? SO ARE YOURS!!

I DON'T WANT YOUR DIRTY DISHES TOUCHING MY DIRTY DISHES!!

YEAH? WELL, I DON'T WANT YOUR GARBAGE TOUCHING MY GARBAGE!!

THAT'S MY PAPER TOWEL! DON'T TOUCH MY PAPER TOWEL!!

IF MOTHERS ONLY KNEW HOW LITTLE THEY HAD TO WORRY ABOUT...

PLEASE LET ME STAY ANOTHER DAY, CATHY. YOU'RE THE ONLY ONE I CAN TURN TO.

OH, NO. I'M NOT FALLING FOR THAT OLD LINE AGAIN.

PLEASE LET ME STAY, CATHY. I WILL NEVER TAKE OUR FRIENDSHIP FOR GRANTED AGAIN.

OH, NO. I'M NOT FALLING FOR THAT OLD LINE AGAIN.

PLEASE LET ME STAY, CATHY. BY HELPING ME, YOU'RE DOING YOUR PART TOWARDS RESTORING ORDER TO THESE TIMES OF ECONOMICAL AND EMOTIONAL CHAOS.

OKAY.

I HADN'T HEARD THAT ONE YET.

MY NEW BOYFRIEND ISN'T SPEAKING TO ME, MY MOM ISN'T SPEAKING TO ME, MY EX-BOYFRIEND IS ASLEEP ON MY COUCH AND I JUST GAINED 8 POUNDS.

OH, CATHY...

THEN AGAIN, MAYBE IT'S NOT SO BAD... SOMETIMES YOU HAVE TO FEEL TERRIBLE BEFORE YOU CAN BE MOTIVATED TO CHANGE SOMETHING.

SOMETIMES YOU CAN ONLY TURN YOUR LIFE AROUND AFTER YOU'VE REALLY HIT THE BOTTOM!

IN WHAT WAY IS A QUART OF ICE CREAM GOING TO HELP?

I'M NOT QUITE LOW ENOUGH.

AREN'T YOU NERVOUS ABOUT IRVING SNOOPING AROUND ALL YOUR STUFF WHILE YOU'RE AT WORK ALL DAY, CATHY?

ANDREA, IRVING AND I HAVE ALWAYS BEEN TOTALLY OPEN ABOUT OUR OTHER FRIENDSHIPS.

I HAVE NOTHING TO HIDE!!

GOOD FOR YOU! AND **WHY** DON'T YOU HAVE ANYTHING TO HIDE?!

I ALREADY HID EVERYTHING.

I TYPED UP THE NOTES FROM THE MEETING YOU MISSED THIS MORNING, CATHY.

THANKS, CHARLENE. I APPRECIATE IT.

5 PEOPLE THINK YOU SHOULD THROW IRVING OUT... 3 PEOPLE THINK YOU SHOULD THROW DAVID OUT...

AND 14 PEOPLE WANT TO COME OVER AND WATCH THEM FIGHT.

I CAN'T BELIEVE THIS! GET BACK IN HERE, CHARLENE!!

WHICH WAY DID YOU VOTE?

DAVID AND IRVING, THIS IS NOT WORKING OUT! I CAN'T POSSIBLY TELL HOW I FEEL ABOUT EITHER OF YOU WHEN BOTH OF YOU ARE HERE!!

AHEM... I ALSO CAN'T TELL HOW I FEEL ABOUT EITHER OF YOU WHEN ONLY ONE OF YOU IS HERE.

I ALSO CAN'T TELL HOW I FEEL ABOUT EITHER OF YOU WHEN BOTH OF YOU ARE GONE. THEREFORE, I AM GOING TO GO WATCH TELEVISION.

NEVER DELIVER A SPEECH WHEN ALL YOU HAVE WRITTEN IS THE FIRST SENTENCE.

MY OFFICE CALLED, IRVING. I HAVE TO GET BACK TO ST. LOUIS.

....WAIT A MINUTE. IF YOU LEAVE, CATHY WILL START MISSING YOU.

WOMEN ALWAYS MISS THE GUY WHO LEAVES FIRST. THIS IS A TRAP!

I HAVE TO LEAVE, IRVING. I HAVE A PLANE.

HAH! I WILL LEAVE FIRST!

I AM LEAVING FIRST!

THEN WE'RE BOTH LEAVING.

GOOD WORK, CATHY. I DIDN'T THINK YOU HAD THE HEART TO TELL THEM BOTH TO GO.

DAVID WENT BACK TO ST. LOUIS AND IRVING MOVED IN WITH HIS PARENTS. AT LEAST MY MOTHER WILL BE THRILLED.

IT WAS HORRIBLE TO SEE THEM LEAVE...BUT I JUST KEPT THINKING, "MOM IS GOING TO BE THRILLED".

SOME THINGS ARE WORTH GOING THROUGH IF ONLY BE-CAUSE YOU KNOW YOUR MOTH-ER WILL BE TOTALLY THRILLED!

...WHATEVER MAKES YOU HAPPY, DEAR.

RELATIONSHIPS ARE LIKE A GIANT PLATE OF SPAGHETTI, ANDREA.

EACH PIECE IS PERFECT BY ITSELF... BUT WHEN YOU PUT IT ALL TOGETHER, IT BECOMES A TANGLED MESS, IMPOSSIBLE TO SORT OUT.

VERY INTEREST-ING, CATHY.

USING THAT SAME THEORY, WE SEE THAT RELATIONSHIPS ARE ALSO LIKE A TINY TOSSED SALAD... AFTER BEING PART OF THE WHOLE, NO ONE PIECE IS EVER EXACTLY THE SAME.

DON'T BE RIDICULOUS.

"AMAZING NEW DIET BREAKTHROUGH! LOSE 15 POUNDS IN 7 DAYS!"

HA! WHAT TRASH!!

GOOD FOR YOU, CATHY. YOU'RE FINALLY GETTING MORE REALISTIC ABOUT YOUR WEIGHT LOSS PROGRAMS!

I NEED TO FIND ONE WHERE I CAN LOSE 15 POUNDS IN 3 DAYS.

WITH OUR NEW VIDEO TAPE RECORDER, WE WATCHED THE 6:00 NEWS AT 8:45. WE SAW YESTERDAY'S 3:00 MOVIE AT 5:20 TODAY.

WE SAW TUESDAY'S 8:00 SPECIAL AT 9:00 SATURDAY MORNING, AND THE 7:30 SUNDAY SYMPHONY DURING LUNCH ON WEDNESDAY.

MOM, THAT'S GREAT TO BE ABLE TO WATCH SHOWS WHEN YOU WANT! WHAT ARE YOU AND DAD GOING TO DO WITH ALL YOUR NEW SPARE TIME?

WE'RE GOING TO TRY TO FIGURE OUT WHAT DAY IT IS.

YOU'RE EATING INSTEAD OF FACING YOUR PROBLEMS AGAIN, CATHY.

WRONG, ANDREA.

EATING HAS A CALMING EFFECT THAT OFTEN ACTUALLY HELPS YOU FOCUS ON YOUR PROBLEMS MORE CLEARLY.

WHEN YOUR MOUTH IS BUSY EATING, IT FREES UP YOUR MIND SO YOU CAN THINK MORE LOGICALLY.

WHAT ARE YOU THINKING ABOUT?

I'M THINKING ABOUT WHAT I CAN EAT NEXT.

I'VE CALLED THIS MEETING TO DISCUSS SOME NEW CONCEPTS IN MANAGEMENT FOR YOUR DEPARTMENTS.

ACCORDING TO THIS STUDY, IF YOUR EMPLOYEES ARE FRUSTRATED, DEPRESSED OR ABSORBED IN PERSONAL PROBLEMS, IT WILL ONLY NEGATIVELY AFFECT OUR CORPORATE GOAL.

IT IS SOMETIMES FAR MORE PRODUCTIVE FOR THESE EMPLOYEES TO ACTUALLY LEAVE THE OFFICE FOR A FEW...

I WASN'T FINISHED YET!!

I WORRY. I THOUGHT, "CATHY MUST BE TOO SICK TO GET TO A PHONE!"

ONLY MY MOTHER COULD MAKE ME FEEL THIS GUILTY.

IS YOUR JOB SO IMPORTANT THAT YOU CAN'T EVEN RE-TURN MY CALLS ANYMORE?!

ONLY A BOYFRIEND COULD MAKE ME FEEL THIS GUILTY.

HOW DO YOU HAVE TIME FOR 14 BOYFRIENDS AND NOT HAVE 3 SECONDS TO CALL ME??!

ONLY A GIRLFRIEND COULD MAKE ME FEEL THIS GUILTY.

BAD NEWS, MOM. YOUR COMPETITION'S GETTING TOUGH.

WHAT DO YOU THINK, CATHY? CAN YOU TURN YOUR JOB INTO SOMETHING MORE, OR WILL YOU CHANGE CAREERS?

SHAMPOO

WHERE DO YOU SEE YOUR-SELF 10 YEARS FROM NOW?

SHAMPOO

WHAT DO YOU THINK ABOUT CHILDREN? REAL ESTATE? RETIREMENT PLANNING?

SHAMPOO

I HAVEN'T EVEN FIGURED OUT IF MY HAIR IS "DRY" "NORMAL", OR "OILY" YET.

SHA

HOW DO YOU KNOW IRVING'S GOING TO PICK A FIGHT?

SIMPLE. HE'S WEAR-ING HIS BLUE-STRIPED SHIRT TODAY.

EVERY TIME IRVING WANTS TO FIGHT HE WEARS HIS BLUE-STRIPED SHIRT. WHEN HE'S GUILTY, HE WEARS HIS YELLOW SWEATER. HE MAKES UP IN TAN, HE BREAKS UP IN GREEN. HE SULKS IN HIS BURGUNDY SWEATSUIT.

MEN ARE SO PREDICTABLE! THEY'RE ABSOLUTELY, TOTAL-LY, 100% PREDICTABLE!!

WHAT ARE YOU CHANGING FOR?

I WANT TO SLIP INTO MY HOLIER-THAN-THOU OUTFIT.

I WON'T BE IN TODAY, MR. PINKLEY. I DON'T THINK I SHOULD BE ALLOWED NEAR A CAR.

I THOUGHT YOU INVITED ME OVER TO SCREAM AT ME, CATHY.

I DID, IRVING.

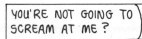

...BUT LISTEN TO THAT SONG ON THE RADIO. REMEMBER HOW HAPPY WE WERE WHEN THAT SONG FIRST CAME OUT?

YOU'RE NOT GOING TO SCREAM AT ME?

NOW THEY'RE PLAYING OUR OTHER FAVORITE SONG! OH, IRVING! IRVING!!

KISS KISS KISS KISS

WHERE'S THE REST OF THE COFFEE, MOM?

I DON'T KNOW. I MADE 3 CUPS.

MOM, "3 CUPS" ON THAT COFFEE MAKER DOESN'T EVEN FILL ONE MUG.

AT MY HOUSE "3 CUPS" MAKES 3 CUPS.

AT YOUR HOUSE YOU USE PUNY CUPS. IF YOU WANT TO MAKE 3 CONTEMPORARY MUGS OF COFFEE, YOU HAVE TO MAKE 7 CUPS!

7 CUPS! WE'LL NEVER FINISH 7 CUPS!!

HOW'S YOUR MOM?

I DON'T KNOW. BY THE TIME WE SAT DOWN TO TALK, WE WEREN'T SPEAKING TO EACH OTHER.

CHARLENE SPENT THE MORNING COMPLAINING ABOUT THE FACT THAT MORRIE NEVER CLEANS UP THE COFFEE ROOM.

THEN JOANN ACCUSED TIM OF STEALING HER IDEAS FOR THE DRAPE PROJECT... THEN BETH ANNOUNCED SHE WAS GOING TO QUIT IF SUE DIDN'T QUIT HOGGING THE WHITE-OUT.

NOW IT'S 4:30 AND YOU'VE BEEN WAITING TO HAVE A MEETING WITH ME ALL DAY... WHAT DID YOU WANT TO DISCUSS, MR. PINKLEY?

CARLA CALLED ME "FATTY"!!

WHY DON'T YOU EVER INVITE ME TO YOUR BUSINESS DINNERS, CATHY?

IRVING, HONEY, IF YOU CAME, I'D SPEND THE WHOLE EVENING WORRYING ABOUT WHETHER OR NOT YOU WERE ENJOYING YOURSELF.

"WHAT'S IRVING THINKING ABOUT?"... "DOES HE FEEL LEFT OUT?"... "IS HE THREATENED?"...

FORGET IT, CATHY. FORGET I EVEN BROUGHT IT UP!!

...WHAT'S IRVING THINKING ABOUT?... DOES HE FEEL LEFT OUT?... IS HE THREATENED?...

I KNOW IRVING AND I ARE TOTALLY DIFFERENT PEOPLE, ANDREA... BUT WE KEEP COMING BACK TO EACH OTHER.

DEEP DOWN, I THINK WE BOTH WANT EXACTLY THE SAME THING!

WE BOTH WANT THE OTHER PERSON TO CHANGE.

CATHY, THEY'VE HAD YOUR CAR FOR 4 DAYS. WHY AREN'T YOU SCREAMING AT THEM?!

IF YOU SCREAM AT THE SERVICE DEPARTMENT THEY PUT YOUR NAME AT THE BOTTOM OF THEIR LIST, ANDREA. BUT WATCH THIS...

HI THERE! HOW'S THE FAMILY? WHEN DO YOU THINK THAT MAGNIFICENT OIL CHANGE MIGHT BE DONE?

SEPTEMBER 22.

THE SERVICE DEPARTMENTS ARE CATCHING ON.

3 TABLESPOONS OF TUNA SALAD AT 193 CALORIES PER 4-OUNCE SERVING... PLUS 2/3 CUP COTTAGE CHEESE AT 260 CALORIES PER CUP... PLUS 1 1/2 OLIVES AT 52 CALORIES PER OUNCE..

...MINUS JOGGING FOR 22 MINUTES, WHICH BURNS OFF 300 CALORIES PER HOUR... MINUS 13 SIT-UPS AT -200 CALORIES PER HOUR...

...EQUALS 21% OF THE MAXIMUM CALORIES ALLOWED TO LOSE WEIGHT AT A RATE OF 2 POUNDS PER WEEK.

WHO GETS THE BILL?

YOU HANDLE IT, ANDREA. I CAN NEVER FIGURE OUT THE TIP.

I'LL BE FINE, MOM. EVERYTHING WILL WORK OUT JUST FINE.

YOUR YOUTH IS SLIPPING AWAY, CATHY. IF YOU DON'T MAKE SOME DECISIONS SOON, THEY'LL BE MADE FOR YOU.

WAAAH! YOU'RE RIGHT! WHAT AM I DOING? WAAAH!!

OH, YOU'LL BE FINE, CATHY. EVERYTHING WILL WORK OUT JUST FINE.

YOU TRICKED ME.

I WAS FEELING LEFT OUT.

IRVING HONEY, I HAVE TO BREAK OUR DATE FOR TO-MORROW NIGHT.

IRVING, MY DARLING HONEY, I HAVE TO BREAK OUR DATE FOR TOMORROW NIGHT.

IRVING, MY DARLING HONEY, WONDERFUL, PRE-CIOUS SWEETIE, I...

THE LONGER I DON'T SAY ANYTHING, THE BETTER YOU GET.

I'VE BEEN CALLED OUT OF TOWN ON BUSINESS. I NEED MY CLOTHES BACK.

YOU JUST BROUGHT THOSE IN AN HOUR AGO.

24-HOUR DRY CLEANING

I KNOW. BUT NOW I NEED THEM BACK.

YOU CAN'T HAVE THEM BACK. THEY'RE FILTHY AND THEY'RE WADDED UP IN A BAG.

GIVE ME BACK MY FILTHY, WADDED-UP CLOTHES!!

FOR WHAT?

I HAVE TO LOOK NICE IN A MEETING.

YOU SHOULD HAVE CHECKED THAT BAG, MISS. IT WON'T FIT UNDER YOUR SEAT.

IT FIT UNDER THE SEAT IN OTHER AIR-PLANES.

IT WON'T FIT UNDER THE SEAT.

I BET I CAN MAKE IT FIT IF I JUMP ON IT.

MISS, WILL YOU AND YOUR TRUNK GET OUT OF THE AISLE? 200 PASSENGERS ARE WAITING BEHIND YOU.

SOME PEOPLE HAVE NO CONSIDERATION.

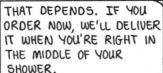

ROOM SERVICE.

HI. I'D LIKE TO ORDER BREAKFAST. HOW LONG WILL IT TAKE?

THAT DEPENDS. IF YOU ORDER NOW, WE'LL DELIVER IT WHEN YOU'RE RIGHT IN THE MIDDLE OF YOUR SHOWER.

HOWEVER, IF YOU ORDER BREAKFAST AFTER YOUR SHOWER, WE'LL WAIT TO BRING IT UNTIL 4 SECONDS BEFORE YOU HAVE TO LEAVE FOR YOUR MEETING.

COULDN'T YOU JUST PLAN TO BRING IT 20 MINUTES FROM NOW?

DON'T BE RIDICULOUS. WE CAN'T TIME THINGS THAT EXACTLY.

THANKS FOR DINNER AND FOR NOT TRYING TO KISS ME, RALPH.

NO PROBLEM. I HAVE A WHOLE NEW RESPECT FOR MY FEMALE BUSINESS ASSOCIATES.

YOU MADE ME REALIZE HOW TACKY IT IS TO EXPECT A KISS IN RETURN FOR BUYING YOU A $50 BUSINESS DINNER.

INSTEAD, YOU CAN REPAY ME BY GIVING AN INFORMAL 45-MINUTE TALK TO 50 OF OUR SALES PEOPLE AT 8:00 TOMORROW MORNING.

EVERY NOW AND THEN, I HATE PROGRESS.

HI, CATHY. HOW'S YOUR TRIP?

AT 10:00 TONIGHT MY CLIENT TOLD ME I WAS SUPPOSED TO GIVE A 45-MINUTE TALK AT 8:00 TOMORROW MORNING, ANDREA.

THEY ONLY GAVE ME ONE NIGHT TO PREPARE A 45-MINUTE TALK FOR 50 PEOPLE!!

ONE NIGHT TO PREPARE WHAT COULD BE THE MOST IMPORTANT PRESENTATION OF MY ENTIRE CAREER!!

OH, CATHY... WHAT ARE YOU GOING TO DO?!

I DECIDED TO GET UP EARLY AND DO IT IN THE MORNING.

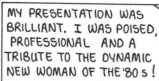

 **Panel 1:** IS THIS THE WARRANTY REGISTRATION CARD YOU'RE SUPPOSED TO SEND IN FOR YOUR PHONE-ANSWERING MACHINE, CATHY?

YES, MOM. HERE. IT GOES IN THIS DRAWER.

 **Panel 2:** YOU STUFF YOUR WARRANTY REGISTRATION CARDS IN A DRAWER??

WHAT DO YOU DO WITH YOURS?

 **Panel 3:** I LET THEM SIT ON THE COUNTER UNTIL I SPILL SOMETHING ON THEM, AND THEN I THROW THEM OUT.

 **Panel 4:** EVERY GENERATION HAS HER OWN SYSTEM.

 **Panel 5:** PLEASE LEAVE A SHORT MESSAGE AFTER THE BEEP...BEEP!

HI. IT'S IRVING...UM... I HAD A GREAT TIME LAST NIGHT AND I..UH.. WELL, UM...I MISS YOU..I.

 **Panel 6:** IRVING, WAIT! MY DARLING! I'M HERE! I'M...

YAAA! YOU WERE LISTENING IN!!

 **Panel 7:** YAAA! YOU LISTENED! FORGET EVERYTHING I SAID! YAAA!! *CLICK*

Panel 8: ...ANOTHER MODERN CONVENIENCE BACKFIRES IN APARTMENT 365.

 **Panel 9:** WE'RE FREEZING, MR. PINKLEY.

 **Panel 10:** IT'S 100° OUTSIDE AND 52° IN THIS OFFICE. WE'RE TOO COLD TO WORK AND WE'RE SICK OF HIDING OUR LOVELY SUMMER OUTFITS UNDER THESE UGLY COATS.

 **Panel 11:** EITHER TURN OFF THE AIR-CONDITIONER OR THE WOMEN IN THIS OFFICE ARE GOING TO MARCH OUT INTO THE SUNSHINE AND YOU CAN...

 **Panel 12:** ...HM! I SEEM TO BE WARMING UP.

I PAID $14.95 FOR THIS DOUBLE ALBUM SET AND I HATE EVERY SONG ON IT BUT ONE.

I'M GOING TO SMASH IT TO PIECES!

CATHY, NO! TAKE IT BACK TO THE RECORD STORE AND MAKE THEM DEAL WITH IT.

HELLO. I PAID $14.95 FOR THAT DOUBLE ALBUM SET AND I HATE EVERY SONG ON IT BUT ONE!!

SMASH!

SEE HOW MUCH MORE SATISFYING IT IS TO WORK WITHIN THE SYSTEM?

I CAN'T TAKE IT, MR. PINKLEY! I'M CRACKING UNDER ALL THIS WORK!!

OH, CATHY. LET ME HELP YOU.

LET'S SEE...YOU HAVE THE DRAPE UPDATE DUE. IS THAT THE PROBLEM?...THERE'S THE McMEEL RESEARCH. THAT DOESN'T LOOK SO BAD...

OH, NO YOU DON'T, MR. PINKLEY.

YOU'RE PURPOSELY BREAKING MY WORKLOAD INTO TINY PIECES SO EACH ONE WILL SEEM INSIGNIFICANT AND DIMINISH THE IMPACT OF THE WHOLE.

HOW DID YOU KNOW THAT?

IT'S THE SAME WAY I EAT A PIE.

YOU LOOK FINE AS YOU ARE.

IT WILL JUST TAKE A SECOND TO CHANGE, IRVING.

...IT'S BEEN 35 MINUTES. I SHOULD LOOK BETTER THAN THIS IF I SPENT 35 MINUTES ON IT.

YAAA! NOW IT'S BEEN 45 MINUTES. HE'S GOING TO BE EXPECTING A MIRACLE AFTER WAITING 45 MINUTES!

CATHY, IT'S BEEN AN HOUR AND A HALF! WHAT ARE YOU DOING IN THERE?!

GO HOME, IRVING.

DEAR FLOYD,
WE ARE SICK AND TIRED OF YOUR OUTRAGEOUS DEMANDS. AS FAR AS I'M CONCERNED, YOU CAN TAKE YOUR BUSINESS AND...

DEAR FLOYD,
THIS IS THE LAST TIME PRODUCT TESTING INC. IS GOING TO CATER TO ONE OF YOUR LUDICROUS EMERGENCIES. IN THE...

DEAR FLOYD,
ENCLOSED ARE THE PROJECTS YOU REQUESTED. BEST WISHES, CATHY.

A GOOD BUSINESS LETTER TAKES SEVERAL DRAFTS.

I'M LOST.

WHAT DO YOU MEAN, YOU'RE LOST, CATHY?

I DON'T KNOW WHERE I BELONG, ANDREA. I'M WITH A PERSON FOR A WHILE, AND THEN I JUST FEEL LOST AGAIN.

EVEN WHEN PEOPLE SAY, "I NEVER WANT TO LOSE YOU," I ALWAYS WIND UP FEELING LOST.

THIS MUST BE WHAT IT FEELS LIKE TO BE A PAIR OF SUNGLASSES.

WHAT DO YOU WANT TO DO IN THE NEXT FIVE YEARS, CATHY?

YOU WERE ALWAYS ON MY MIND... YOU WERE ALWAYS ON MY MIND...

I WOULD LIKE TO SPEND THE NEXT FIVE YEARS STARING AT YOUR GORGEOUS FACE.

I'M SORRY... I COULDN'T HEAR YOU OVER THE MUSIC.

UM... I'D LIKE TO SPEND THE NEXT FIVE YEARS EXPLORING THE MANY FASCINATING ASPECTS OF MY CAREER.

OH.

ANOTHER RELATIONSHIP GETS DROWNED OUT BY A LOVE SONG.

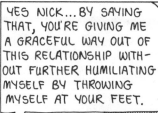

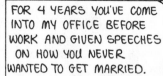

HOW COULD CHARLENE MARRY A MAN LIKE FRANK? I THOUGHT SHE'D MADE MORE PROGRESS THAN THAT.

CATHY, FRANK IS EXACTLY THE TYPE OF GUY THAT IRVING IS, AND YOU'VE DATED HIM FOR 5 YEARS!

WHAT PROGRESS DO YOU THINK YOU'VE MADE??

I'M LESS TOLERANT OF MY FRIENDS' RELATIONSHIPS.

BZZZ BZZZ BZZZZZ BZZZZ

YOU'RE STILL HERE??

DON'T YOU HAVE ANYWHERE ELSE TO GO? DON'T YOU HAVE SOMETHING ELSE TO DO??

BZZZ BZZZZ BZZZ

YOU HAVE THE WHOLE WORLD TO PICK FROM!! WHY ARE YOU TORTURING ME??

BZZZZ BZZZZZ BZZZZ

COMPANY ALWAYS STAYS TOO LONG IN AUGUST.

BZZZ BZZZ BZZZ BZZZ

IRVING.....

AACK. I CAN'T SAY THAT. I'LL SOUND SO CONFUSED AND WEAK.

I AM CONFUSED. BUT IT'S SO EMBARRASSING TO ADMIT IT. I'M SCARED TO SAY I CARE. I'M SCARED TO SAY I DON'T.

AAAGH. THIS IS AGONY! THIS IS TORTURE TO OPEN UP TO HIM...

IRVING, I THINK WE NEED TO DISCUSS OUR RELATIONSHIP.

SURE YOU DO. IT'S SO EASY FOR WOMEN TO TALK ABOUT THEIR FEELINGS.

NICK DUMPED ME, MOM.

GOOD RIDDANCE, NICK, YOU MISERABLE SCUM !!!

HE WAS VERY NICE...

OH, NICK... WE MISS YOU, NICK !!

MAYBE HE FELT THREATENED BY IRVING.

PHOOEY ON YOU, IRVING ! YOU RUIN EVERYTHING !!!

NO, THAT'S NOT IT. IRVING'S BEEN WONDERFUL...

YOU'RE GIVING YOUR MOTHER A HEADACHE, CATHY.

ONE HUNDRED AND... WAIT. I DON'T THINK THE SCALE WAS EXACTLY ON ZERO WHEN I GOT ON.

NOPE. IT WAS A TEENSY BIT OVER ZERO. THE SCALE MUST START **EXACTLY ON ZERO** OR THE READING ISN'T ACCURATE... NO, IT'S STILL A FRACTION OVER... NO... NO....

...THERE !

CATHY, THAT WAS AT LEAST 5 POUNDS **UNDER** ZERO WHEN YOU GOT ON !

I GOT TIRED OF TRYING TO FIX IT.

I WAS JUST IN A RELATIONSHIP WHERE I DID ALL THE WORK, IRVING. IT'S YOUR TURN.

MY TURN ?? I WASN'T IN YOUR LAST RELATIONSHIP.

I KNOW... BUT IN THE BIG PICTURE OF MEN AND WOMEN, IT'S THE **MAN'S** TURN TO PUT OUT THE EFFORT AND **MY** TURN TO BE PAMPERED AND ADORED.

WHAT ??

GO AHEAD, IRVING. FLATTER ME. CHARM ME. BEG ME TO BE YOURS LIKE I BEGGED NICK TO BE MINE !!

BLEAHHH !

WHERE'S IRVING ?

THERE'S AN OUTSIDE CHANCE THAT HE WENT TO BUY ME A GIFT.

OUR MOTHERS JUST DIDN'T TALK ABOUT THINGS, CATHY.

I KNOW. WHEN MY MOM IS REALLY UPSET ONE OF HER FINGERS MOVES A LITTLE... BUT THAT'S IT.

Coffee to go

THEY WERE CONDITIONED TO KEEP EVERYTHING INSIDE.

HER WHOLE RAGE ON A SUBJECT COMES OUT AS ONE TINY, NERVOUS MOVE OF ONE FINGER.

THANK HEAVENS OUR GENERATION IS BEYOND THAT!

HOORAY FOR US!!

WE'VE LEARNED TO USE OUR ENTIRE HAND.

I READ A STORY ABOUT A WOMAN MY AGE WHO STARTED A COMPANY AND IS MAKING $200,000 A YEAR. I RAN HOME AND ATE A BOX OF DONUTS.

I TALKED TO A FRIEND WHO'S GROVELLING AROUND TRYING TO FIGURE OUT WHAT TO DO WITH HER LIFE. I CHARGED OVER TO MY OFFICE AND FINISHED 4 PROJECTS.

OUT

IN

WHEN SALLY WAS MADE A VICE PRESIDENT, I ATE A CARTON OF COOL-WHIP... ...WHEN PAM GOT FIRED, I WROTE A BRILLIANT, 20-PAGE RESEARCH REPORT.

I'M RESPONDING TO ALL THE WRONG ROLE MODELS.

ARE YOU SURE YOU CAN'T STAY FOR AWHILE, IRVING? MY MOTHER BROUGHT OVER THIS GREAT PIE.

NO... I'D BETTER GET GOING, CATHY.

ARE YOU SURE? IT'S JUST DELICIOUS, AND THERE'S A GREAT MOVIE ON LATER.

NO. THANKS, BUT I REALLY HAVE TO GO.

CATHY, IT'S ME. I CHANGED MY MIND.

KNOCK KNOCK

YOU'RE WORKING LATE? YOU PROMISED YOU'D HELP PLAN MY DINNER PARTY.

I'M SORRY, MOM. NEXT WEEK I'LL COOK THE WHOLE DINNER AND HELP YOU CLEAN YOUR ENTIRE HOUSE.

YOU'RE WORKING LATE? WHAT ABOUT THE PAMPHLETS YOU SAID YOU'D HELP ME MAIL?

I'M SORRY, ANDREA. NEXT WEEK I'LL HAND-DELIVER THE PAMPHLETS WITH A PERSONAL NOTE OF APOLOGY TO EACH ONE.

YOU'RE WORKING LATE? I THOUGHT WE WERE GOING TO SEE A MOVIE.

I'M SORRY, IRVING. NEXT WEEK I'LL TAKE YOU TO EVERY MOVIE IN TOWN AND I'LL WAX YOUR CAR.

...JUST THINK, CATHY. WHEN THIS WEEK IS OVER, YOU CAN JUST SIT BACK AND RELAX!

IF YOU DON'T GET THE PROJECT DONE, YOU'LL UNDERMINE YOUR CLIENT'S TRUST AND RISK LOSING THE BUSINESS THAT PAYS YOUR SALARY, CATHY.

THEN AGAIN, IF YOU **DO** GET THE PROJECT DONE, YOU'LL HAVE SET A PRECEDENT FOR SPEED THAT WILL HAUNT YOU THE REST OF YOUR CAREER AND GIVE YOU A NERVOUS BREAKDOWN.

IF YOU GET THE PROJECT DONE BUT DO IT POORLY BECAUSE YOU'RE HURRYING, YOU'LL DEMEAN YOUR CAPABILITIES AND DESTROY ALL CHANCE FOR ADVANCEMENT.

I LOVE A JOB WITH AN ELEMENT OF SUSPENSE.

WELL, HERE WE ALL ARE: COFFEE TO HELP ME STAY AWAKE... COOKIES TO HELP ME WRITE...

DONUTS TO HELP ME TYPE... PRETZELS TO HELP ME PROOFREAD... CHOCOLATE TO HELP ME COLLATE...

HOW'S IT GOING, CATHY?

MY STAFF KEEPS DISAPPEARING.

-61-

MY CAR SEATS LEAN ALL THE WAY BACK. ALMOST LIKE A BED.

HM. WHAT A LOVELY CHOCOLATE COLOR.

THIS SOFA IS A HIDEAWAY. YOU BELIEVE IT? THIS BEAUTY TURNS INTO A BED!

WHAT AN INTERESTING PATTERN. LIKE MILLIONS OF LITTLE OREOS.

OF COURSE, THIS CHAIR IS AS COMFORTABLE AS A BED! THERE'S ROOM FOR 2 ON HERE!

WELL, LOOK AT THAT! THAT LEATHER IS THE EXACT HUE OF THE INSIDE OF A MILK DUD!

TWO ONE-TRACK MINDS ON DIFFERENT TRACKS.

HERE, SWEETIE. IF YOU FOLDED YOUR TOWELS LIKE THIS, YOUR LINEN CLOSET WOULD BE SO MUCH MORE EFFICIENT!

I LIKE THE WAY I DO IT, MOTHER.

YOU COULD ALWAYS KEEP YOUR BILLS IN THIS LITTLE BASKET, AND THEN THEY WOULDN'T GET STREWN ALL OVER THE HOUSE!

I HAVE MY OWN SYSTEM, MOTHER.

ARRANGE PACKAGED PRODUCTS BY DATE OF PURCHASE, AND YOU'LL ALWAYS KNOW WHAT'S FRESH!

I'M A GROWN WOMAN! I DON'T NEED YOU TO TELL ME HOW TO RUN MY HOUSE!

WHAT'S WRONG WITH THIS SOAP, CATHY?

IT ISN'T THE KIND MY MOM ALWAYS BUYS.

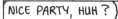

NICE PARTY, HUH?

IT WAS HORRIBLE! WHENEVER SUE FEELS JEALOUS OF MY JOB, SHE GETS BACK BY THROWING HERSELF AT YOU LIKE THAT.

SUE WAS THROWING HERSELF AT ME??

OH, COME ON, IRVING... PLUS, BILL WASN'T SPEAKING TO JAN, SO JAN SPENT THE NIGHT FLIRTING WITH SUE'S BOYFRIEND, JOE.

YOU'RE KIDDING! I DIDN'T SEE THAT!

HOW ABOUT WHEN BILL'S OLD GIRLFRIEND SHOWED UP WITH HER NEW HUSBAND, WHO I USED TO DATE?

IT WAS ONE OF THE MOST TENSE, EMBARRASSING, AWKWARD EVENINGS OF MY LIFE!

WOMEN ALWAYS HAVE A BETTER TIME AT THESE THINGS THAN MEN DO.

THIS IS THE HOT NEW LOOK IN TWEEDY JACKETS FOR FALL...

FALL FASHION HEADQ...

AND THIS IS THE HOT NEW LOOK IN SKIRTS...

FALL FASHI HEAD

...PUT THEM TOGETHER WITH THE HOT NEW LOOK IN SWEATERS AND TEXTURED HOSE. IT'S HOT, HOT, HOT!

...BOY, DO YOU LOOK HOT, CATHY!

THANK YOU.

TICKETS

MORE SHOES? WHAT DO YOU NEED MORE SHOES FOR, CATHY?

WOMEN'S SHOES

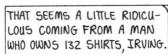

THAT SEEMS A LITTLE RIDICULOUS COMING FROM A MAN WHO OWNS 132 SHIRTS, IRVING.

WOMEN

...NOT TO MENTION THE FACT THAT MEN'S SHIRTS ESSENTIALLY STAY IN STYLE FOR YEARS, WHEREAS WOMEN'S SHOES CHANGE RADICALLY EACH SEASON... THE QUALITY AND CUT OF WHICH ARE OFTEN THE BASIS BY WHICH A WOMAN'S ENTIRE PRESENCE IS JUDGED!

I HATE IT WHEN THE DEFENSE IS PREPARED.

WOMEN SHOES

I DON'T SEE WHY YOU WON'T LET ME FIX YOU UP, CATHY.

ANDREA, WAIT! DON'T EAT THAT TUNA SALAD! IT'S ROTTEN.

IF IT'S ROTTEN, WHAT'S IT DOING IN YOUR REFRIGERATOR?

WELL, IT'S NOT THAT ROTTEN...I MEAN, I'VE SORT OF GOTTEN USED TO SEEING IT IN THERE.

I COME HOME FROM WORK EVERY DAY AND THERE IT IS... A FAMILIAR FACE...A FRIEND...SOMEONE TO TALK..

ARE YOU SURE YOU DON'T WANT TO GET FIXED UP?

WHO EXACTLY DO YOU KNOW?

FLOYD AND HELEN, MARGO AND JACK, AND NEIMAN-MARCUS ARE CELEBRATING THEIR ANNIVERSARIES TODAY. I'M SENDING THEM ALL A NICE CARD.

NEIMAN-MARCUS IS A STORE, MOM.

THEY'VE BEEN TOGETHER 75 YEARS!

FOR 75 YEARS THEY'VE STAYED COMMITTED TO THEIR RELATIONSHIP, UNLIKE YOU YOUNG PEOPLE TODAY WHO BREAK UP BEFORE YOU EVEN KNOW EACH OTHER'S LAST NAMES!

I GET THE POINT, MOTHER.

POINT? WHAT POINT? I WAS JUST MAKING CONVERSATION.

WHY DID I TELL PINKLEY I'D WORK ON THAT STUPID PROJECT THIS WEEKEND??

WHY CAN'T I LOSE ANY WEIGHT? WHY AREN'T I SAVING ANY MONEY? WHY DO I LISTEN TO ANDREA'S ADVICE?

AND **YOU**, IRVING! WHY DO YOU ALWAYS DISAPPEAR JUST WHEN THINGS ARE STARTING TO WORK??

CLEANING THE HOUSE CAN BE VERY THERAPEUTIC.

MR. PINKLEY SAID YOU'D FILL ME IN ON THE NEW PERSON HE HIRED FOR MY DEPARTMENT.

HE'S SINGLE, CATHY! SINGLE, SINGLE, SINGLE!!

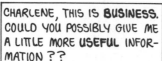

CHARLENE, THIS IS **BUSINESS**. COULD YOU POSSIBLY GIVE ME A LITTLE MORE **USEFUL** INFORMATION??

SORRY.

HE'S 5'10", WITH A POWERFUL YET LEAN WARREN BEATTY BODY, A PAUL SIMON SMILE, A TUMBLE OF SUN-STREAKED WALNUT HAIR, AND EYES THE COLOR OF A 1979 STEEL BLUE MERCEDES BENZ 450 SL.

THANK YOU.

CATHY, I'D LIKE YOU TO MEET GRANT. HE'LL BE WORKING DIRECTLY UNDER YOU.

HEE HEE

WHAT IS THE MATTER WITH ME??

BLEEBLE BLEEBLE HEE HEE HEE

NICE MEETING YOU TOO, CATHY.

A NEW WORLD RECORD: FIVE YEARS OF PROGRESS, DOWN THE DRAIN IN FOUR SECONDS.

WHO ARE YOU ALL DOLLED-UP FOR, CATHY? YOUR NEW ASSISTANT, GRANT???

CHARLENE, IF YOU EVEN HINT TO GRANT THAT I USUALLY DON'T LOOK THIS NICE, THE ENTIRE OFFICE IS GOING TO HEAR ABOUT YOU AND THE WORD PROCESSOR MAINTENANCE MAN.

OPEN YOUR MOUTH ABOUT THAT MAINTENANCE MAN AND PINKLEY'S GOING TO KNOW WHO STEALS THE FIG NEWTONS FROM HIS TOP DRAWER.

ONE WORD ABOUT THOSE FIG NEWTONS AND I GO STRAIGHT TO YOUR FIANCÉ WITH...

NEVER MIND.

THERE'S NOTHING LIKE NEGOTIATING A BIG DEAL BEFORE 8:30 IN THE MORNING.

I'M STARVING. WANT TO GET SOME LUNCH, CATHY.?

UM... I DON'T THINK IT'S A GOOD IDEA, GRANT.

DID YOU ALREADY EAT?

NO, BUT IF I LEAVE THE OFFICE WITH YOU, EVERYONE WILL ASSUME IT'S A DATE.

BELIEVE ME, THE SICK, CONTRIVING MINDS IN THIS OFFICE WILL TURN AN INNOCENT TUNA SANDWICH BETWEEN YOU AND ME INTO THE ROMANCE OF THE CENTURY!!

WHO WOULD DO SOMETHING LIKE THAT?

I WOULD.

THERE ARE 7 MILLION MORE SINGLE ADULT WOMEN IN THIS COUNTRY THAN THERE ARE SINGLE ADULT MEN.

I SPEND 99% OF MY LIFE AT WORK. HOWEVER, I'M NOT SUPPOSED TO DATE ANYONE IN MY COMPANY.

WHAT, THEN, IS MY CHANCE OF MEETING AN AVAILABLE, ATTRACTIVE MAN IN MY 1% OF REMAINING TIME WHO SHARES AN INTEREST IN THE THINGS I DO, YET WORKS IN A TOTALLY DIFFERENT FIELD?

... I ALWAYS KNEW THOSE STORY PROBLEMS WOULD COME BACK TO HAUNT ME.

YESTERDAY GRANT SAID THE...

CATHY, FORGET GRANT. YOU ARE NOT GOING TO DATE SOMEONE WHO WORKS IN YOUR OFFICE.

DO YOU REALIZE HOW HIDEOUS IT WOULD BE IF YOU AND GRANT BROKE UP AND YOU STILL HAD TO SEE HIM EVERY DAY??

I BROKE UP WITH IRVING 5 YEARS AGO, AND I STILL SEE **HIM** EVERY DAY.

I REST MY CASE.

I'M GLAD YOU CHANGED YOUR MIND ABOUT DATING SOMEONE AT WORK.

THIS ISN'T A DATE, GRANT. WE'RE SITTING IN MY OFFICE.

CATHY, IT'S 9:00 AT NIGHT, WE'RE EATING DINNER, BRUCE SPRINGSTEEN IS SINGING IN THE BACKGROUND, AND WE'RE TALKING ABOUT THE PEOPLE WE'RE GOING TO GO OUT WITH.

YES, AND UNFORTUNATELY, SINCE WE'RE NOT GETTING ANYTHING DONE, WE'RE GOING TO HAVE TO WORK LATE AGAIN TOMORROW NIGHT!

OH, DARN.

DARN, DARN DARN...

Panel 1: YOU'RE FINALLY CLEANING OUT THIS CLOSET??

WELL, I THOUGHT, WHAT IF GRANT ASKS ME OUT AND I SAY "YES".

Panel 2: THEN WHAT IF WE HAVE SUCH A WONDERFUL TIME THAT HE BEGS TO COME OVER AND FIX ME DINNER THIS WEEKEND... AND WHILE HE COOKS, I LEAN OVER AND WHISPER ENDEARING THINGS IN HIS EAR...

Panel 3: FLUSTERED BY MY COOL CHARM, HE KNOCKS THE HOLLANDAISE SAUCE ON THE FLOOR AND GOES LOOKING FOR A RAG TO CLEAN IT UP... IF THAT HAPPENED, I WOULD WANT THIS CLOSET TO BE NICE AND NEAT.

Panel 4: THIS IS PATHETIC, CATHY.

IT'S GETTING THE CLOSET CLEAN, ISN'T IT?

Panel 5: SOMEONE FROM THE OFFICE IS GOING TO SEE US HERE, GRANT.

YOU'RE SO PARANOID, CATHY.

Panel 6: YOU'RE NOT PARANOID?

CATHY, I DON'T CARE WHAT ANYONE IN THE OFFICE THINKS.

Panel 7: SO WHAT IF THEY SEE US?? LET THEM SEE US! LOOK!! CATHY AND GRANT ARE...

EXCUSE ME...

Panel 8: READY TO ORDER, SWEETHEART?

Panel 9: WHAT MAKES YOU SUCH AN EXPERT ON DATING SOMEONE AT THE OFFICE, MOM?

I SAW IT ON THE PHIL DONAHUE SHOW.

Panel 10: PHIL POINTED OUT THAT OFFICE DATING PUTS A HIDEOUS STRAIN ON BOTH YOUR WORK AND RELATIONSHIP, AND THE AUDIENCE CHEERED!

Panel 11: THEN PHIL SAID, "BUT COULDN'T A LOVING, DISCREET COUPLE MAKE IT WORK?", AND THE AUDIENCE CHEERED THAT... THEN PHIL GOT EXASPERATED BECAUSE THE SAME PEOPLE KEPT CHEERING FOR OPPOSITE THINGS, AND THE AUDIENCE CHEERED THAT! THEN...

Panel 12: WHAT'S YOUR POINT, MOM?

I FORGOT.

THIS REPORT YOU DID IS ALL WRONG, GRANT... WELL, IT ISN'T **THAT** WRONG. NO. YES, IT IS. IT'S WRONG.

GRANT, I CAN'T DO THIS. WE ARE NOT GOING OUT ANYMORE. YOU HAVE TO RE-DO THIS WORK AND FORGET ABOUT GOING OUT.

WE ARE NEVER GOING OUT AGAIN. DO YOU WANT TO GO OUT TONIGHT AND TALK ABOUT IT??

WHY DOES THE WOMAN ALWAYS HAVE TO BE THE STRONG ONE?

GRANT'S PHONE IS BUSY. THAT'S AN OMEN THAT I SHOULDN'T BE CALLING HIM.

MY HAIR IS TANGLED. THAT'S AN OMEN THAT I SHOULDN'T BE GOING OUT WITH HIM TODAY.

HE'S 3 MINUTES LATE, AN OMEN THAT THIS WHOLE RELATIONSHIP IS OUT OF SYNC.

IT'S POURING OUT, CATHY. MAYBE WE SHOULDN'T BE GOING TO THE GAME TODAY.

MEN ARE SO SUPERSTITIOUS.

I LOVE GETTING TO SEE YOU IN THE OFFICE EVERY DAY, CATHY.

ME TOO, GRANT. BUT NO ONE ELSE CAN FIND OUT ABOUT US.

NO ONE ELSE WILL EVER KNOW.

WE'LL GO OUT AT NIGHT, BUT AT THE OFFICE IT'S STRICTLY BUSINESS!

THEY'LL NEVER EVEN SUSPECT WE'RE DATING!

OH, GRANT! IT WILL BE OUR OWN BEAUTIFUL SECRET!!

LAURA WAS BEAUTIFUL... I WANT TO MEET SOMEONE AS BEAUTIFUL AS LAURA, AND AS BRIGHT AS MAUREEN.

I'M BEAUTIFUL. I'M BRIGHT.

I WANT SOMEONE AS WITTY AS JOAN, AS SENSITIVE AS KAREN, AS CHARMING AS SUE.

I'M WITTY. I'M SENSITIVE. I'M CHARMING.

I WANT...

ME! WHAT ABOUT ME? YOU IDIOT! ME! ME!!

NAH. TOO HYSTERICAL.

THIS IS WHAT MEN HATE, CATHY. I WENT WITH YOU A COUPLE OF TIMES, AND SUDDENLY YOU'RE MAKING ME FEEL THE PRESSURE OF A WHOLE RELATIONSHIP.

WE DON'T HAVE A RELATIONSHIP. WE HAD TWO GREAT DATES. WHO KNOWS? MAYBE WE'LL GO OUT AGAIN.

BUT UNTIL WE DO, I AM NOT GOING TO KISS THE GROUND YOU WALK ON, OR FEEL SOME HUGE GUILT BECAUSE I'M NOT DANCING THROUGH EVERY MOMENT OF MY LIFE WITH YOU!

WHAT DID GRANT SAY?

"GREAT DATES. GO OUT AGAIN. KISS AND DANCE."

IN THE 70'S WE USED TO LEAP INTO LOVE BUT THEN DENY THAT WE WERE INVOLVED.

NOW IT'S THE 80'S. WE TALK ABOUT HOW MUCH WE WANT TO GET INVOLVED, BUT WE STAY A MILE AWAY FROM AN ACTUAL RELATIONSHIP.

WERE WE BETTER OFF CARING AND PRETENDING WE DIDN'T, OR ARE WE BETTER OFF ADMITTING WE WANT TO CARE, EVEN THOUGH WE RUN WHEN THE OPPORTUNITY PRESENTS ITSELF?

...THIS MAY BE A TWO-CAKE QUESTION.

WHAT WERE YOU DOING SO LATE AT THE OFFICE, CATHY?

WHY? ARE YOU JEALOUS, IRVING?

WHY? WOULD YOU LIKE IT IF I WERE JEALOUS?

WHY? IF I SAID I LIKED IT, WOULD YOU FEEL MANIPULATED?

WHY? IF I FELT MANIPULATED, WOULD YOU ACCUSE ME OF OVER-REACTING?

WHY? IF I SAID YOU OVER-REACTED, WOULD YOU TAKE ME IN YOUR ARMS AND SMOTHER ME WITH KISSES??

HUH?

THE BEST DEFENSE IS A GOOD OFFENSE.

IRVING'S NEVER GOING TO SPEAK TO ME AGAIN...

NAH... IT ISN'T THAT BAD. WE'VE HAD A LITTLE SETBACK. THAT'S ALL... NOPE. THIS IS IT. THINGS DON'T GET ANY WORSE THAN THIS.

...NAH. THINGS WERE WORSE THAN THIS IN 1976. THIS IS NOTHING. JUST RIDE IT OUT AND IT WILL STABILIZE...

WHAT ARE YOU DOING, CATHY?

I'M TRYING TO DECIDE IF I'M IN A DEPRESSION OR A RECESSION.

GRANT WAS SUPPOSED TO BE HERE AT 8:00.

HE'S LATE. DUMP HIM.

DUMP HIM? MOM, IT'S ONLY 8:07.

DUMP HIM!

WAIT, MOM... HERE HE IS.

HELLO AND WELCOME TO DUMP-CITY, GRANT!!

DING DONG

HEE HEE... BLEEBLE BLEEBLE, HEE HEE...

SOMEHOW, IT'S REAS-SURING TO SEE WHERE MY PERSONALITY CAME FROM.

IT'S 8:00, CATHY. AREN'T YOU GOING HOME TONIGHT?

NOT YET, CHARLENE. I HAVE SO MUCH WORK TO DO!

REPORTS TO PREPARE... NUMBERS TO GO OVER... DICTATING TO CATCH UP ON... I COULD BE HERE FOREVER!

GRANT ALREADY LEFT. HE SNEAKED OUT THE BACK DOOR TWO HOURS AGO.

GOODNIGHT, CHARLENE.

I ALWAYS USED TO GET MY DAD A TIE FOR HIS BIRTHDAY.

BUT NOW I'M MUCH MORE AWARE OF THE NEW "FATHERING" ROLE. THE MORE I READ ABOUT THE "SHARING AND NURTURING" FATHER...

...THE MORE I APPRECIATE THE IMPACT MY DAD HAD ON ME, AND HOW FAR AHEAD OF HIS TIME HE WAS IN THE WAY HE BROUGHT ME UP!!

SO NOW WHAT ARE YOU GOING TO GET HIM?

A TIE. BUT A MORE MEANINGFUL TIE.

I'M FURIOUS WITH GRANT ABOUT OUR DATE LAST NIGHT, BUT I DON'T WANT HIM TO THINK THAT'S WHY I'M CRITICIZING HIS REPORT.

I JUST HAVE TO BE DIGNIFIED, PROFESSIONAL, AND CHOOSE MY WORDS VERY CAREFULLY.

DRIVEL! DRIVEL! DRIVEL!!

...HM! IT WASN'T AS HARD AS I THOUGHT.

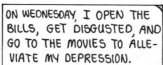

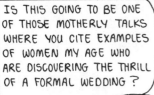

Panel 1: WHAT ARE YOU DOING WHILE GRANT'S OUT OF TOWN? / I'M STARVING MYSELF ON A HIDEOUS DIET...

Panel 2: ...TORTURING MYSELF WITH EXERCISES...AND ATTACKING MY FACE, HAIR, AND NAILS WITH BEAUTY TREATMENTS SO I'LL BE GORGEOUS WHEN HE GETS BACK.

Panel 3: CATHY, THIS IS PATHETIC. IF YOU HAD LEFT TOWN, GRANT WOULD BE USING THIS WEEK TO GO OUT WITH EVERYONE IN THE CITY. / THAT'S WHAT MAKES WOMEN SO SPECIAL, ANDREA.

Panel 4: ...WE'RE CAPABLE OF ENTERTAINING OURSELVES.

Panel 5: THESE DIET BREAKFAST SQUARES ARE DISGUSTING. I SHOULD HAVE GONE ON THE CAMBRIDGE DIET TODAY... BLEAH.. THIS IS WORSE. I SHOULD HAVE GONE ON THE BEVERLY HILLS DIET...

Panel 6: BLEAH. I'LL NEVER STAY ON THIS. I SHOULD HAVE STARTED THE SCARSDALE DIET. NO. WAIT.. BLEAH. I'LL GO ON THE STILLMAN.. WAIT.. NO.. THE ATKINS... THE..YEECH.. THE...

Panel 7: WHAT AM I DOING HERE ?? FOR ONCE, WHY DON'T I JUST GO ON A SENSIBLE REDUCTION PROGRAM WHERE I RECORD EVERYTHING I EAT?!

Panel 8: ...BREAKFAST: 13,000 CALORIES.

Panel 9: DIET DIARY ENTRY, THURSDAY, 9:00 A.M.: "RADICAL CHANGES IN DIET ARE TOO BIG A SHOCK TO THE SYSTEM. IT IS FAR BETTER TO SIMPLY CUT DOWN ON FATTENING FOODS."

Panel 10: CHOMP!

Panel 11: CHOMP! CHOMP! CHOMP! CHOMP! CHOMP!

Panel 12: DIET DIARY ENTRY, THURSDAY, 9:06 A.M.: "CUTTING DOWN NEVER WORKS."

I ATE A DONUT. AFTERWARDS, I REALIZED MY URGE FOR THAT DONUT WAS JUST A MANIFESTATION OF MY JOB ANXIETY.

I ATE A BOX OF COOKIES. AFTERWARDS, I REALIZED THE COOKIES WERE JUST A SYMBOLIC COMPENSATION FOR MY INABILITY TO MAINTAIN A FULFILLING RELATIONSHIP.

I ATE A CARROT. I REALIZED NOTHING.

WHY DO I ONLY GET PHILOSOPHICAL AFTER I'VE EATEN SOMETHING FATTENING?

I HAVE 42 LETTERS TO GET OUT THIS MORNING, AND ALL I CAN THINK ABOUT IS THE DONUT I SAW ON CHARLENE'S DESK.

I GET AS FAR AS "DEAR MR. COOPER," AND THEN THAT DONUT POPS INTO MY MIND..... GET OUT OF MY MIND, DONUT!!

I AM IN CHARGE HERE!! YOU ARE NOT GOING TO RUN MY LIFE, YOU MISERABLE LITTLE DONUT!!

"DEAR MR. COOPER, REGARDING YOUR BUDGET, WE HAVE PAID SPECIAL ATTENTION TO THE LITTLE COLORED SPRINKLES ON THE THICK FUDGE FROSTING..."

HOW'S THE DIET, CATHY?

I HAD A BLUEBERRY MUFFIN ONE INCH FROM MY MOUTH, CHARLENE... BUT I RAN INTO THE BATHROOM AND THREW IT DOWN THE TOILET!

I HAD AN UNWRAPPED CANDY BAR IN MY HANDS... I CRUSHED IT TO PIECES AND THREW IT DOWN THE TOILET!!

I WAS SECONDS AWAY FROM A CHEESE DANISH! I SQUASHED IT WITH MY STAPLER AND THREW IT DOWN THE TOILET!!

THAT'S TERRIFIC, CATHY! LET ME KNOW IF THERE'S ANYTHING I CAN DO.

CALL MAINTENANCE.

—80—

TWO YEARS AGO YOU BOUGHT A JUMP ROPE. YOU SAID, "IF I'VE INVESTED $5, I'LL USE IT." YOU DIDN'T.

LAST YEAR YOU BOUGHT A SWEATSUIT AND A WORKOUT ALBUM. YOU SAID, "IF I'VE INVESTED $60, I'LL USE THEM." YOU DIDN'T.

NOW YOU'RE GOING TO BUY A $500 MEMBERSHIP IN A HEALTH CLUB?? CATHY, WHAT ARE YOU THINKING??

THE OLDER I GET, THE MORE IT COSTS TO MAKE ME FEEL GUILTY.

OH, YES. OUR HEALTH CLUB HAS COMPLETELY SEPARATE FACILITIES FOR MEN AND WOMEN.

WONDERFUL.

SEPARATE WORK-OUT ROOMS... SEPARATE DRESSING AREAS... SEPARATE INSTRUCTORS...

WONDERFUL.

ANY OTHER QUESTIONS?

HOW AM I SUPPOSED TO GET IN THE FRONT DOOR?

HEALTH CLUB

CATHY, HOW DID YOU LOSE 10 POUNDS IN 4 DAYS??

NEW FAT IS EASIER TO LOSE THAN OLD FAT, ANDREA.

IT'S ALL TIMING. IF YOU GAIN 5 POUNDS IN ONE NIGHT, YOU COULD LOSE IT IN 2 DAYS. BUT IF YOU WAIT A WEEK, FORGET IT.

AFTER A WEEK, THE NEW FAT HAS ALREADY BECOME PART OF YOUR BODY'S FAT FAMILY AND IT'S...

...SOMETIMES I HATE THE THINGS I'M AN EXPERT ON.

OF ALL THE NEUROTIC BEHAVIOR I'VE SEEN, GRANT, THIS TAKES THE CAKE.

I CANNOT BELIEVE A GROWN MAN WOULD **HIDE** RATHER THAN FACE A SIMPLE RELATIONSHIP DISCUSSION!!

IRVING'S IN THE LOBBY, CATHY. HE WANTS TO KNOW WHERE YOU'VE BEEN FOR THE LAST MONTH.

MOVE OVER, GRANT.

IF YOU'RE TRYING TO GET ME TO BREAK UP FIRST SO YOU WON'T HAVE IT ON YOUR CONSCIENCE, FORGET IT, GRANT. I CAN OUTLAST YOU ANY DAY!! A WOMAN CAN DRAG OUT A BREAK-UP LONGER THAN ANY MAN!!

...GET OUT OF HERE, GRANT! IT'S OVER BETWEEN US!!

HM! I USED TO HAVE MORE STAMINA THAN THAT.

I THOUGHT WE SHOULD INCLUDE EVERYONE. FAMILY, FRIENDS, CO-WORKERS. THEN NO ONE WOULD FEEL LEFT OUT.

BUT GRANT SAID, "NO. LET'S KEEP IT PRIVATE...TELL OUR BEST FRIENDS, AND THEN WE CAN SEND ANNOUNCEMENTS TO EVERYONE ELSE." BUT I...

CATHY, YOU MEAN YOU'RE...

BREAKING UP, MOM. WE'RE PLANNING OUR BREAK-UP.

ANOTHER DAY, ANOTHER 5000 GREY HAIRS.

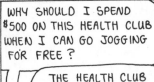

WHY SHOULD I SPEND $500 ON THIS HEALTH CLUB WHEN I CAN GO JOGGING FOR FREE?

THE HEALTH CLUB PROVIDES A FAR MORE COMPLETE EXERCISE PROGRAM.

HEALTH CLUB & FITNESS CENTER

NEW MEMBERS

NAH...

THE HEALTH CLUB AMBIANCE IS A POWERFUL PSYCHOLOGICAL MOTIVATOR TO KEEP YOU WORKING TOWARDS YOUR GOALS.

HEAL CLU & FITN CENT

NEW MEMB

NAH...

THE HEALTH CLUB IS A CENTER FOR INTELLIGENT, SUCCESSFUL, GORGEOUS, MUSCLE-Y MEN.

BINGO.

SIGN RIGHT HERE.

NEW M

NOW THEN... YOU SAID, "THE HEALTH CLUB IS A CENTER FOR INTELLIGENT, SUCCESSFUL, GORGEOUS, MUSCLE-Y MEN."

CORRECT.

BY THAT DID YOU MEAN INTELLIGENT MEN, SUCCESSFUL MEN, GORGEOUS MEN, AND MUSCLE-Y MEN? FOUR DIFFERENT TYPES OF MEN?

HEALTH CLUB & FITNESS CENTER

NEW MEMBER

OR DID YOU MEAN THE CLUB IS A CENTER FOR MEN WHO HAVE ALL FOUR OF THESE QUALITIES IN ONE?? OR DID YOU MEAN THAT SOME OF THE MEN HAVE SOME OF THESE QUALITIES??

HEL CLU & FIT CEN

NEW M

I NEVER SIGN A CONTRACT UNTIL I UNDERSTAND ALL THE FACTS.

THERE'S JUST A TOUCH OF STUFFING LEFT. WHO WILL CLEAN IT UP SO WE CAN STACK THESE PLATTERS?

IF SOMEONE WOULD EAT THAT LAST BLOB OF POTATOES, WE WOULDN'T HAVE TO DIRTY UP ANOTHER FOOD STORAGE CONTAINER.

LOOK AT THIS PIE. WHO'LL HAVE ANOTHER SLIVER SO WE CAN EVEN OFF THE PIE?

WE'RE FAT, BUT WE'RE NEAT.

AS PART OF OUR HEALTH CLUB PROGRAM, EACH NEW MEMBER GETS A FREE INTRODUCTORY ANALYSIS.

NOW THEN, WHAT ARE YOUR PROBLEM AREAS?

WHAT ARE YOUR FITNESS GOALS?

DO YOU HOPE TO GAIN OR LOSE WEIGHT?

NONE OF YOUR BUSINESS.

THAT'S PRIVATE.

HAH!

I SEE. WELL, LET'S JUST TAKE A FEW...

DON'T COME NEAR ME WITH THAT TAPE MEASURER, YOU TOOTHPICK!!

WHAT DID YOU LEARN IN YOUR ANALYSIS, CATHY?

NEVER GO TO THE HEALTH CLUB THE DAY AFTER THANKSGIVING.

THE SECOND I TELL MYSELF I CAN'T HAVE ANY CAKE, I GET OBSESSED WITH HAVING SOME. IT'S RIDICULOUS.

I'LL BET IF SOMEONE PUT A CAKE IN FRONT OF ME AND TOLD ME TO EAT IT, I WOULDN'T EVEN WANT IT.

WOULD YOU LIKE A PIECE OF CAKE, CATHY?

YES!

NEVER TRUST A DIETING MIND.

CATHY, DIDN'T YOU DO **ANY**-THING DURING THE 6 WEEKS YOU WERE SEEING GRANT??

NO.

I'M 6 WEEKS BEHIND ON WORK, BILLS, LAUNDRY, CLEANING... I'VE LOST TOUCH WITH MY PARENTS AND MY FRIENDS.

IT'S ACTUALLY A RELIEF TO HAVE THAT RELATIONSHIP OVER WITH SO I CAN GET BACK TO MY NORMAL LIFE.

...IRVING!!

YOU'VE HAD 6 WEEKS TO YOURSELF, SWEETIE.. ..YOU'D BETTER BE READY TO SPEND SOME TIME WITH ME!

TO THE ANDREWS FAMILY... WISHING YOU A WARM AND WONDERFUL CHRISTMAS. I HOPE 1983 WILL BE A SPECIAL YEAR FULL OF LOVE AND PROSPERITY.

TO THE BURKOFF FAMILY... BEST WISHES FOR A VERY MERRY CHRISTMAS AND THE HAPPIEST OF NEW YEARS.

DEAR DIGGS FAMILY... MERRY CHRISTMAS, HAPPY NEW YEAR.

DEAR SALEMS... MERRY CHRISTMAS.

DEAR WILSONS... GREETINGS.

PEOPLE TOWARD THE END OF THE ALPHABET DON'T GET MUCH IN THE WAY OF CHRISTMAS NOTES.

BUY ONE OF THESE NEW POUFFY TAFFETA DRESSES AND YOU'LL BE THE CENTER OF ATTENTION AT ALL YOUR HOLIDAY FUNCTIONS!

I SEE WHAT YOU MEAN.

THERE WILL ONLY BE ROOM FOR ONE OTHER PERSON AT EVERY PARTY.

OKAY. I LIED. I DIDN'T GO OUT OF TOWN.

I WAS AFRAID YOU'D YELL AT ME IF I JUST TOLD YOU I WAS TOO BUSY.

LOOK, **LOTS** OF THINGS ARE IMPORTANT TO ME. I PROMISE TO FIND MORE TIME IN THE FUTURE, BUT NOT THE WEEK BEFORE CHRISTMAS!

BRAVO, CATHY! WHAT DID IRVING SAY??

THAT WASN'T IRVING. IT WAS MY AEROBICS TEACHER.

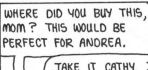
WHERE DID YOU BUY THIS, MOM? THIS WOULD BE PERFECT FOR ANDREA.

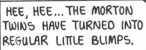
TAKE IT, CATHY. I HADN'T DECIDED WHO TO GIVE IT TO.

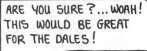
ARE YOU SURE?...WOAH! THIS WOULD BE GREAT FOR THE DALES!

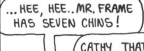
TAKE IT, SWEETIE. I CAN GET ANOTHER ONE.

REALLY?...OOH! WHAT'S THIS?

IRVING WOULD LOVE THIS!

THIS IS GORGEOUS!

TAKE IT!

TAKE IT!

TAKE IT!

A MOTHER'S SHOPPING IS NEVER DONE.

HEE, HEE...THE MORTON TWINS HAVE TURNED INTO REGULAR LITTLE BLIMPS.

MOM, THAT'S TERRIBLE!

...HEE, HEE..MR. FRAME HAS SEVEN CHINS!

CATHY, THAT'S TERRIBLE!

...HEE, HEE..WHAT HAPPENED TO MARTHA'S HAIR??!

HEE, HEE, HEE! OH, WHAT FUN!

WHY DON'T **WE** EVER SEND OUT PHOTO CHRISTMAS CARDS?

I'D BETTER TASTE THE DOUGH. I CAN'T TELL IF IT'S RIGHT UNLESS I TASTE IT.

NOW I HAVE TO TASTE A PARTIALLY DONE COOKIE TO MAKE SURE THE BATCH IS BAKING PROPERLY.

NOW I MUST TASTE THE COOLED COOKIES TO MAKE SURE THEY AREN'T OVER OR UNDER-COOKED!!

PERFECTIONISTS TEND TO BE OVERWEIGHT.

A PRACTICAL GIFT TELLS HIM THE ROMANCE IS OVER. A PERSONAL GIFT TELLS HIM THE ROMANCE HAS JUST BEGUN.

AN INTIMATE GIFT SAYS YOU WANT TO GET CLOSER. A KITCHEN GIFT SAYS YOU WANT HIM TO CHANGE. A SPORTS GIFT SAYS YOU WANT HIM TO THINK YOU UNDERSTAND HIM.

A HAND-MADE GIFT SAYS, "I'M SWEET AND HOMEY"... AN EXPENSIVE GIFT SAYS, "I'M INDEPENDENT AND WORLDLY AND AWARE!!"

WHAT DID YOU DECIDE TO GET IRVING?

THE GIFT OF CONFUSION.

AS EACH GIFT IS OPENED, FATHER WILL NEATLY FOLD THE GIFT WRAP FOR RE-USE, AND I WILL RECORD WHO EACH PRESENT IS FROM SO WE'LL HAVE A COMPLETE LIST FOR OUR THANK YOU NOTES!

Merry Christmas

...NOT BAD. AT LEAST THIS YEAR I HAD TIME TO GET MY WHOLE SPEECH OUT.

MORE PIE? MORE COOKIES? MORE STRUDEL? MORE NUT BREAD? MORE CANDY?

THERE ARE DEEP, PSYCHOLOGICAL REASONS FOR WHY MOTHERS STUFF THEIR CHILDREN WITH FOOD OVER THE HOLIDAYS, MOM.

I KNOW, CATHY.

IF I FATTEN YOU UP, YOU'LL BE TOO EMBARRASSED TO LEAVE THE HOUSE, SO YOU'LL STAY LONGER!

...SO MUCH FOR INTROSPECTION.

I WISH YOU DIDN'T HAVE TO GO RUSHING OFF TO SEE IRVING, SWEETIE.

YOU'RE RUSHING OFF?

I'M NOT RUSHING OFF.

IF IRVING'S SO WONDERFUL, WHERE WAS HE WHEN YOU HAD MEASLES IN THE 1st GRADE?

I THOUGHT YOU BROKE UP WITH IRVING.

YOU'RE LEAVING THE PARENTS WHO LOVE YOU TO EXCHANGE GIFTS WITH A MAN YOU BROKE UP WITH??

DOES IRVING HAVE A JOB YET? DOES IRVING HAVE A FUTURE??

...I KNOW, SWEETIE! WHY DON'T YOU JUST HAVE IRVING COME OVER HERE?!

CLICK! CLICK!

THE SUITCASE IS COMING OUT. CATHY'S GETTING READY TO LEAVE.

YAAACK! THE SUITCASE IS OUT! THE SUITCASE IS OUT!!!

I HATE YOU, YOU STUPID SUITCASE!!

...AND MOTHERS WONDER WHY WE WAIT UNTIL THE LAST SECOND TO PACK.

DO YOU THINK CATHY HAD A GOOD TIME WITH US OVER CHRISTMAS?

WHY? JUST BECAUSE YOU ASKED ABOUT HER LOVE LIFE EVERY TEN MINUTES?

HOW ABOUT WHEN I TOLD HER TO RINSE HER DIRTY DISHES OR THERE'D BE NO DESSERT? THAT REALLY BUGGED HER!

HA, HA! THEN I GAVE HER MY ANNUAL INVESTMENT LECTURE! SHE HATES THAT!

HOO, HA! DID YOU SEE HER FACE WHEN I WHIPPED OUT MY CARTON OF CLIPPINGS?!

HOO, BOY! THEN THE CAR DISCUSSION... THEN THE HAIR DISCUSSION... WHAT A VISIT!!

NOT MANY FAMILIES COULD PACK SO MUCH INTO SIX SHORT DAYS.

FIND OUT WHAT YOU DID AT THE OFFICE HOLIDAY PARTY

PRICES: $5 AND UP

DO YOU ACTUALLY EXPECT ME TO PAY $5 TO READ GOSSIP ABOUT MYSELF, CHARLENE?

NO. BUT I THOUGHT YOU'D PAY $15 TO READ ABOUT PINKLEY, OR $25 FOR GRANT.

IN FACT, I THOUGHT YOU MIGHT EVEN GO THE FULL $89.95 FOR THE COMPLETE BOUND SET: "THE 1982 OFFICE PARTY IN REVIEW"!

A SMART RETAILER KNOWS HER CUSTOMERS.

FIND OUT WHAT YOU DID AT THE OFFICE HOLIDAY PAR

PRICES: $5 AN

IF I BUY A PIE AT THE 7-11 AT MIDNIGHT ON JANUARY 5TH, EVERYONE WILL KNOW I'M CHEATING ON MY NEW YEAR'S DIET.

SO WHAT? WHAT DO I CARE IF THE CASHIER AT THE 7-11 THINKS I'M CHEATING ON MY DIET?? HAH!

HELLO I WOULD LIKE TO BUY THIS PIE AND I DON'T CARE WHAT YOU THINK!!!

WHAT'S HAPPENED TO YOUR DIET, CATHY?

MY STRONG SIDE KEEPS SHOWING UP AT THE WRONG TIME.

WHY ARE YOU MAKING SUCH A BIG DEAL ABOUT RETURNING THE MAKE-UP BAG YOU GOT FOR ANDREA?

SOME SALESPERSON WAS COUNTING ON THE COMMISSION FROM THIS, MOM.

OH, FOR HEAVEN'S SAKE, CATHY. EVERYONE RETURNS THINGS AFTER CHRISTMAS.

HI. I'D LIKE TO RETURN THIS.

CALL EDITH AND TELL HER TO CUT THE VACATION SHORT! HER MAKE-UP BAG SALE JUST FELL THROUGH!!

HAPPY MOTHER'S DAY, MOM.

YOU SHOULDN'T HAVE.

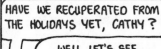

Panel 1: HAVE WE RECUPERATED FROM THE HOLIDAYS YET, CATHY?

WELL, LET'S SEE... TODAY BRIAN ACCUSED FRANK OF STEALING HIS ACCOUNT...

Panel 2: MARK ACCUSED JACK OF STEALING HIS GIRLFRIEND...PAM ACCUSED JOE OF STEALING HER CELERY... AND CHARLENE SPENT THE MORNING SCREAMING AT EVERYONE FOR REFUSING TO ATTEND THE NEW COPIER DEMONSTRATION.

Panel 3: OUT OF A COMPANY OF 45 PEOPLE, ONLY 3 ARE ACTUALLY SPEAKING TO EACH OTHER.

Panel 4: AT LAST! THINGS ARE FINALLY BACK TO NORMAL!

Panel 5: IRVING'S BEEN GONE FOR A WEEK AND HE HASN'T CALLED ONCE.

THEN THIS IS PROBABLY HIM.

RING RING!

Panel 6: WHAT DO I SAY? SHOULD I ACT MAD? SHOULD I LET HIM KNOW I'M HURT?

RING RING!

Panel 7: SWEETIE, JUST PICK UP THE PHONE AND SAY THOSE THREE MAGIC LITTLE WORDS.

RING RING!

Panel 8: IS SHE SKINNY?!

Panel 9: EARLIER TODAY YOU TURNED DOWN A 15¢ DONUT, A 35¢ COOKIE, AND A 50¢ CUPCAKE...

Panel 10: ...AND NOW YOU'RE DIVING INTO A $10.00 BOX OF GOURMET CHOCOLATES.

Panel 11: CATHY, HOW COULD YOU **DO** THIS TO YOURSELF??!

Panel 12: I WAS HOPING THE MORE EXPENSIVE FAT WOULD LOOK BETTER ON ME.

WE HAVE THE AUTO-REDIAL TELEPHONE WITH 9, 15, OR 32-NUMBER MEMORY... THE ALL-ELECTRONIC MINI-PHONE... CORDLESS, COLLAPSIBLE OR CALCULATOR PHONES...

PHONES WITH A MUTE SWITCH, RINGER ON/OFF SWITCH, AND/OR AMPLIFIER SWITCH. PHONES THAT WILL ANSWER, RECORD, TIME CALLS OR TURN ELECTRICAL APPLIANCES ON OR OFF FROM ANYWHERE IN THE WORLD!

DO YOU HAVE ANY PHONES THAT WILL NOT RING SO MUCH AT THE OFFICE, BUT WILL RING MORE AT HOME?

NO.

ONCE AGAIN, MODERN TECHNOLOGY ZOOMS PAST THE OBVIOUS.

PHONE CENTER

WHAT HAPPENED HERE?!

I STUFFED MY PHONE BILL DOWN THE GARBAGE DISPOSAL AND IT BROKE.

THAT WILL BE $42.00.

$42.00?? BLAAAA!!

RIP!!

APARTMENT 365: HOME OF THE DAILY COMPOUNDED DEBT.

YOU SEEM TO INTUITIVELY KNOW HOW TO HANDLE THE OZWELL CLIENT, CATHY. PLEASE CALL AND EXPLAIN WHY WE'RE $12,000.00 OVER BUDGET.

I HAVE ALWAYS FOUGHT FOR WOMEN'S RIGHTS. WANT TO COME OVER AND SEE MY FILE OF CORRESPONDENCE WITH PRO-WOMAN LEGISLATORS??

I LOVE AND RESPECT YOU ENOUGH TO KNOW YOU NEED TIME TO YOURSELF, MY DARLING. BYE.

MEN ARE REALLY STARTING TO CHANGE, AREN'T THEY?

YES. THEY'RE GETTING SNEAKIER.

 THIS SHOWER CURTAIN IS DISGUSTING. THE SECOND I GET HOME FROM WORK, I'M GOING TO DISINFECT THIS SHOWER CURTAIN!

 THIS CLOSET IS DISGUSTING. THE SECOND I GET HOME FROM WORK, I'M GOING TO ORGANIZE THIS CLOSET!

 THIS CAR IS DISGUSTING. THE SECOND I GET HOME FROM WORK, I'M GOING TO CLEAN OUT THIS CAR!!

 PLEASE MAKE ME WORK LATE TONIGHT, MR. PINKLEY.

 ONE FOR DINNER. DINING ALONE, MISS? HOW ABOUT THIS PUNY TABLE NEXT TO THE KITCHEN?

 MAY I HAVE A MENU, PLEASE? HEY SAM! THE LADY WITH NO DATE WANTS A MENU!!

 CHECK! I'VE BEEN WAITING 45 MINUTES FOR MY CHECK!! WHAT'S THE MATTER? AFRAID YOU'RE GOING TO MISS OUT ON SOME SHOPPING TIME??

 ...ISN'T THAT JUST LIKE A WOMAN TO NOT LEAVE A DECENT TIP??

 ...SO THE SHIPMENT DIDN'T COME, LEAVING ME WITH... IRVING, HONEY, TONIGHT IS MY "COMPLAINT NIGHT," REMEMBER?

 WHAT ARE YOU TALKING ABOUT? YOU BEEFED ABOUT YOUR JOB FOR TWO HOURS LAST NIGHT. I WAS JUST SHOWING COMPASSION FOR YOUR COMPLAINT. LAST NIGHT WAS YOURS.

 TONIGHT WE SHARE IN MY PROBLEMS!!!

 I DON'T KNOW HOW MANY MORE YEARS OF THE "US DECADE" I CAN TAKE.

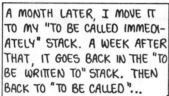

I KNOW WHERE EVERY LADIES' ROOM IN THE CITY IS.

I CAN LOOK AT A RACK OF 700 KINDS OF PANTYHOSE AND MAKE MY SELECTION IN TWO SECONDS FLAT!

I KNOW SIX WAYS TO RE-HEM A SKIRT WITHOUT THREAD... ..AND WITH THE ENTIRE WORLD CRASHING AROUND ME, I'M ABLE TO FOCUS ON ONE SPLIT-END FOR UP TO AN HOUR!!!

HOW'S THE RESUME COMING?

NOT BAD. SO FAR, I'M "INFORMED, DECISIVE, RESOURCEFUL AND DILIGENT."

SO, UM.. HOW LONG HAVE YOU BEEN IN THE COMMODITIES FIELD?

WELL, I...

ONE ORDER OF POTATO SKINS SMOTHERED WITH BACON BITS, CHEESE AND SOUR CREAM...

I WANT TO GO HOME NOW.

ME TOO.

FIRST DATES LASTED LONGER WHEN THEY USED TO SERVE LITTLE PRETZEL STICKS.

MY OLD BUDDY, ZACK, SPLIT UP WITH HIS WIFE AND ASKED IF HE COULD HANG OUT HERE.

THAT'LL BE NICE FOR YOU, IRVING.

NICE?! I'VE WAITED FOUR YEARS FOR THIS! MY DRINKING BUDDY'S BACK! MY CAROUSING BUDDY! ZACK!!

YEOOWCH!!

IS IT MY IMAGINATION, OR DID SOMEONE JUST BITE ME IN THE KNEE?

REMEMBER WHEN WE USED TO CRUISE THIS MALL AND CHECK OUT THE LADIES, IRVING?

DON'T TORTURE ME, ZACK.

WHAT WOMAN IS GOING TO LOOK AT A COUPLE OF GUYS WITH A 2-YEAR-OLD?

A BABY! A BABY!!

LET ME HOLD HER.

IT USED TO BE ALL A GUY NEEDED TO ATTRACT THE LADIES WAS A SPORTS CAR. I COULD HANDLE THAT.

THEN PLANTS. A GUY WITH A FICUS BENJIMINA AND A $2,000 STEREO SYSTEM HAD IT MADE.

...BUT NOW I DON'T SEEM "WITH IT" UNLESS I HAVE A 2-YEAR-OLD AND A BRIEF-CASE FULL OF TOYS. CATHY, HOW AM I SUPPOSED TO DO THAT??!

OH, IRVING...

PATHOS. THE UNIVERSAL CHARMER.

IN MODERN PARENTING, WE LEARN THAT A CHILD'S ACTIONS ARE ALWAYS MOTIVATED, IRVING.

SPLAT!

BECKY SENSES YOUR HOSTI-LITY TOWARDS HER, AND IS EXPRESSING HER FRUSTRATION BY THROWING FOOD AT YOU.

SPLAT!

I SEE BECKY'S IN THE FOOD-FLINGING STAGE.

ALSO A POSSIBILITY.

IRVING FLAKED-OUT ON VALENTINE'S DAY AGAIN? WHY DON'T YOU JUST SCREAM AT HIM, CATHY??

NO GOOD, ANDREA. I DID THAT LAST VALENTINE'S DAY.

HOW ABOUT THE SILENT TREATMENT??

NOPE. I DID THE SILENT TREATMENT IN 1977 AND 1980.

HOW ABOUT THE OLD GUILT-TORTURE APPROACH?!

NOPE. I USED THAT IN 1978, 1979 AND 1981.

THE LONGER YOU DATE SOMEONE, THE HARDER IT IS TO KEEP THINGS FRESH.

ECONOMY CLASS IS $592.

BUSINESS CLASS IS $745.

$592?! WHAT A RIP-OFF!

$745?! OUTRAGEOUS!

AND FIRST CLASS IS $1186.

$1186?! ARE YOU OUT OF YOUR MIND?!

GOOD MORNING. YOU'VE BEEN ASSIGNED THE CENTER SEAT, SURROUNDED BY SCREAMING BABIES AND AIR-SICK ADULTS.

FLIGHT 65

GROUCH CLASS.

AFTER EVERYTHING WE'VE BEEN THROUGH TOGETHER, I CAN'T BELIEVE YOU'D TURN ON ME LIKE THIS.

I WAS ONLY GONE FOR TWO DAYS, AND LOOK AT YOU. YOU'RE A WRECK!

SOMETIMES I WISH I'D NEVER MET YOU!!

MY DESK AND I JUST BROKE UP.

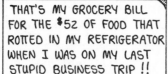

I WON'T BE IN TODAY, MR. PINKLEY. MY HAIR WON'T START.

WHERE ARE THEY?! WHERE ARE ALL THE SINGLE MEN?!!

STANDING ON YOUR BALCONY SCREAMING ISN'T GOING TO HELP, CATHY.

YOU'LL ONLY MEET SOMEONE NEW WHEN YOU JUST RELAX AND DO THE THINGS YOU NORMALLY DO.

THAT IS WHAT I NORMALLY DO.

I WILL NOT ASK CATHY ABOUT HER LOVE LIFE.

I WILL NOT YELL AT MOM FOR DROPPING BY UNINVITED.

I WILL NOT LECTURE CATHY ABOUT HER MESSY APARTMENT.

I WILL NOT BE ANNOYED BY THE 20 CLIPPINGS MOM BROUGHT OVER.

THE CONVERSATION REALLY SLOWS DOWN WHEN WE'RE CONTROLLING OURSELVES, DOESN'T IT?

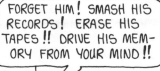

HI THERE. I WAS ADMIRING YOU FROM ACROSS THE ROOM AND WONDERED IF I COULD BUY YOU A DRINK...

ME?? YES! I'VE WAITED ALL MY LIFE FOR A WOMAN TO ASK ME OUT! YES! BUY ME A DRINK! BUY ME DINNER!

BUY ME A CAR AND A HOUSE! YES! YA HA!! I AM ALL YOURS!!!

I CHANGED MY MIND.

YOU WALKED RIGHT UP AND ASKED ME OUT FOR A DRINK! I LOVE IT!!

OF COURSE, A "DRINK" IS THE IDEAL FIRST DATE. IF THE OTHER PERSON TURNS OUT TO BE OBNOXIOUS AND DISGUSTING, YOU'RE NOT STUCK WITH HIM FOR THE WHOLE EVENING.

WELL, I DON'T FIND YOU OBNOXIOUS AND DISGUSTING! SO HOW ABOUT IF WE STAY ON FOR DINNER??

I HATE QUESTIONS LIKE THAT.

MY GOAL IS TO MARRY AN AMBITIOUS CAREER WOMAN SO I CAN SPEND THE REST OF MY DAYS PERFECTING MY MUSCLE TONE.

SHE WILL WORK. I WILL JOG. SHE WILL COOK. I WILL LIFT WEIGHTS. SHE WILL CLEAN. I WILL ADMIRE MYSELF IN FULL-LENGTH MIRRORS!!

WHAT'S YOUR GOAL, CATHY?

MY GOAL IS TO REMEMBER WHAT YOU SAID LONG ENOUGH TO TELL MY GIRLFRIEND WHEN I GET HOME.

HOW WAS THE BIG DATE LAST NIGHT, CATHY?

MOM, I'M A GROWN, INDEPENDENT WOMAN.

I HARDLY THINK I NEED TO GIVE YOU A REPORT ON EVERY DATE.

CATHY, IF YOU'RE SO INDE-PENDENT, WHY DID YOUR MOTHER EVEN KNOW YOU HAD A DATE LAST NIGHT??

IT SLIPPED OUT WHEN SHE WAS BEGGING ME TO IRON AND HEM HER DRESS.

I'LL HAVE THE 7-SUMMER VEGETABLE SOUP AND A BUCKWHEAT MUFFIN.

I'LL HAVE THE NUT-AND-SEED PATTY AND A SMALL, UN-STRAINED CARROT JUICE.

I'M GOING TO NEED A LITTLE TIME TO MYSELF TONIGHT, BRIAN.

I UNDERSTAND, CATHY. YOU WANT SOME QUIET TIME TO REFLECT ON OUR NEW RELATIONSHIP.

I WANT TO GO EAT A BANANA SPLIT.

BRIAN HAS NO JOB, NO AM-BITION, AND NO PERSONALITY. I'M DATING HIM STRICTLY FOR HIS LOOKS.

SO WHAT? YOU OWE IT TO YOUR-SELF, CATHY.

YOU OWE IT TO YOURSELF TO BUY A NEW OUTFIT FOR A GREAT-LOOKING GUY! YOU OWE IT TO YOURSELF TO SPLURGE ON NEW COLOGNE FOR A GREAT-LOOKING GUY!!

AND YOU OWE IT TO YOUR-SELF TO TAKE THAT GREAT-LOOKING GUY OUT ON THE TOWN!!!

EVERY TIME YOU SAY, "I OWE IT TO MYSELF," I WIND UP OWING AMERICAN EXPRESS ANOTHER $50.

PHONE CALLS. THERE ARE TOO MANY PHONE CALLS.

RING RING RING!

HOW AM I SUPPOSED TO GET ANY WORK DONE WITH ALL THESE PHONE CALLS ??!!

YOU DIDN'T GET ANY PHONE CALLS THIS MORNING, CATHY.

I KNOW. I WAS LISTENING IN ON YOURS.

ON SUNDAY I TOLD IRVING I HAD TO STAY HOME AND DO THE LAUNDRY. BUT I REALLY WENT OUT WITH BRIAN.

ON MONDAY I TOLD IRVING I HAD TO PAY BILLS...I WENT OUT WITH BRIAN. ON TUESDAY I TOLD IRVING I HAD TO CLEAN... I WENT OUT WITH BRIAN.

TONIGHT IRVING'S COMING OVER. WHAT AM I GOING TO TELL HIM??

WHY DO YOU HAVE TO TELL HIM ANYTHING, CATHY?

I HAVE A FEELING HE'S GOING TO SUSPECT SOMETHING.

BILLS

IRVING SAID, "HOW COULD YOU GO OUT WITH HIM?!" I SAID, "OH DARLING, I WAS THINKING OF YOU EVERY MOMENT."

YOU DIDN'T SAY THAT, CATHY...

...YOU SCREAMED AT IRVING FOR SNOOPING INTO YOUR AFFAIRS AND HE STORMED OUT OF YOUR APARTMENT!

DIARY

I CAN'T BELIEVE YOU'RE SITTING THERE CHANGING A CONVERSATION YOU ALREADY HAD!!

DIARY

AS LONG AS I'M GOING TO LIVE IN THE PAST, I MIGHT AS WELL IMPROVE IT.

DIARY

Panel 1

WE ASSERTED OUR INDEPEN-DENCE IN TIGHT, STRAIGHT SKIRTS AND BUTTONED VESTS.

Panel 2

WE REAFFIRMED OUR FEMI-NINITY IN MINI-SKIRTS AND SEE-THROUGH TOPS.

Panel 3

NOW WE ARE SALUTING OUR INDEPENDENT YET FEMININE HEALTHY BODIES IN DAZZLING LEOTARDS AND TIGHTS.

Panel 4

EVERY TIME WOMEN ENTER ANOTHER PHASE, THERE'S A WHOLE NEW CATEGORY OF CLOTHES I CAN'T GET INTO.

Panel 5

BUTTON UP YOUR BLOUSE, SWEETIE. YOU DON'T WANT TO GIVE THE WRONG IMPRES-SION.

OH, FOR HEAVEN'S SAKE, MOTHER. THIS IS 1983.

Panel 6

NEVER BE PUSHY. PUSHY WOMEN ARE VERY UN-ATTRACTIVE.

MOM, THIS IS BUSINESS. I **HAVE** TO BE PUSHY TO GET AHEAD.

Panel 7

PUT THE ROLL DOWN, DEAR. YOU HAVE POTATOES COMING WITH YOUR MEAL.

THERE IS NOTHING WRONG WITH ONE ROLL.

Panel 8

CATHY! I CAN'T BELIEVE A WHOLE WEEK HAS SLIPPED BY SINCE I TALKED TO YOU!

NEITHER CAN I, MOM...

Panel 9

SHAMPOO I TRIED ONCE AND HATED... COLOGNE I'VE GOTTEN SICK OF... FACE CREAM THAT DIDN'T WORK...

Panel 10

MAKEUP THAT'S THE WRONG COLOR... HAIR CLIPS THAT WON'T STAY IN MY HAIR... BUBBLE BATH THAT I'M ALLER-GIC TO...

Panel 11

MY BATHROOM CUPBOARDS ARE FILLED WITH THINGS I WILL NEVER USE, FORCING ME TO THROW THE THINGS I **DO** USE ALL OVER THE COUNTER!

Panel 12

THE FAMILY TRADITION LIVES ON!!

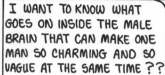

CAN I GET YOU ANYTHING ELSE? YES. I WANT ANSWERS.

I WANT TO KNOW WHAT GOES ON INSIDE THE MALE BRAIN THAT CAN MAKE ONE MAN SO CHARMING AND SO VAGUE AT THE SAME TIME??

WHAT IS IT MEN WANT AND WHY DON'T THEY JUST SAY IT INSTEAD OF PUTTING US THROUGH THIS TORTURE GUESSING GAME THAT DESTROYS OUR SELF-CONFIDENCE AND PERSONALITIES?!

MOVE OVER.

I WISH I'D MET YOU BEFORE, CATHY. YOU WOULDN'T HAVE LIKED ME BEFORE, BRIAN. I HAD NO SELF-ESTEEM.

I USED TO COOK FOR MY DATE, CLEAN FOR MY DATE, IRON FOR MY DATE, DO WHAT MY DATE WANTED TO DO, THINK THE WAY MY DATE THOUGHT...

I USED TO LIVE MY WHOLE LIFE FOR THE PERSON I WAS DATING!!

NOW I REALLY WISH I'D MET YOU BEFORE.

MILK, $2.14 A HALF GALLON... COFFEE CREAM, 59¢ A PINT... ORANGE JUICE, $1.98 A QUART...

TOMATO JUICE, 99¢ A CAN... DIET POP, $2.19 A SIX-PACK ... MINERAL WATER, $1.03 A BOTTLE...

...FOR A GRAND TOTAL OF $32.18.

HI, CATHY. WHERE HAVE YOU BEEN? I JUST LIQUIDATED MY ASSETS.

MY FRIEND FLO'S DAUGHTER'S EX-ROOMMATE SAW CATHY HAVING DINNER WITH IRVING TONIGHT AND CATHY DID NOT LOOK HAPPY.

FLO CALLED THE JOHNSTON FAMILY, WHO ALERTED LOUISE, WHO CALLED MARTHA, WHO CALLED JOAN, WHO WIRED SUSAN, WHO FINALLY TRACKED ME DOWN AT THE MARKET...

CATHY, SWEETIE... TELL YOUR MOTHER WHAT'S WRONG!!

MOM! HOW DID YOU KNOW??

SOME DAYS MOTHERLY INTUITION TAKES MORE OF US THAN OTHERS.

WHAT SHOULD I SAY IF IRVING ASKS ME OUT?

IF HE ASKS YOU OUT FOR FRIDAY NIGHT, IT MEANS YOU'RE SECOND CHOICE. TELL HIM NO.

IF HE ASKS YOU OUT FOR SATURDAY NIGHT, IT MEANS HE PROBABLY JUST BROKE UP WITH SOMEONE AND WILL TRY TO MOLD YOU INTO HIS EX-GIRLFRIEND. TELL HIM NO.

ALL THE "WINNERS" OF FRIDAY AND SATURDAY NIGHT GET DISPLAYED AT SUNDAY BRUNCH. IF HE ASKS YOU OUT FOR SUNDAY BRUNCH, TELL HIM NO!

...SUDDENLY, I'M STARTING TO WISH IT WAS MONDAY.

ANGER EVENTUALLY PASSES. FRUSTRATION GOES AWAY. EVEN LOVE CAN DISAPPEAR.

WHY IS IT THAT ONLY EM- BARRASSMENT STAYS EXACT- LY AS INTENSE FIVE YEARS LATER AS IT WAS THE MOMENT YOU WERE FIRST EMBARRAS- SED ABOUT SOMETHING??!

...AND WHY DO I KEEP RE-PROVING THAT THEORY?